Policing Hat

Policing Hate

Have we abandoned freedom and equality?

Joanna Williams

CIVITAS

First published
December 2020

© Civitas 2020

55 Tufton Street
London SW1P 3QL

email: books@civitas.org.uk

ISBN 978-1-912581-21-4

Independence: Civitas: Institute for the Study of Civil
Society is a registered educational charity (No. 1085494)
and a company limited by guarantee (No. 04023541).
Civitas is financed from a variety of private sources to
avoid over-reliance on any single or small group of donors.

All the Institute's publications seek to further its objective
of promoting the advancement of learning. The views
expressed are those of the authors, not of the Institute.

Typeset by Typetechnique

Printed in Great Britain
by 4edge Limited, Essex

Contents

Author

Joanna Williams is director of the Freedom, Democracy and Victimhood Project at Civitas. Previously she taught at the University of Kent where she was Director of the Centre for the Study of Higher Education. Joanna is the author of *Women vs Feminism* (2017), *Academic Freedom in an Age of Conformity* (2016) and *Consuming Higher Education, Why Learning Can't Be Bought* (2012). She co-edited *Why Academic Freedom Matters* (2017) and has written numerous academic journal articles and book chapters exploring the marketization of higher education, the student as consumer and education as a public good. In addition, Joanna has written about education, feminism and gender for many popular outlets including *The Spectator, The Sun, The Telegraph* and *American Conservative*. Joanna is a regular columnist for the online magazine Spiked.

Summary

Hate crime, and legal restrictions on hate speech, broadly defined, have a long history. Blasphemy laws, passed in the Medieval Period, were not fully rescinded until earlier this century. The Race Relations Act (1965) prohibited 'incitement to racial hatred'. Since this time, myriad new offences have been created, primarily through amendments to Public Order and Criminal Justice Acts. The law specifies additional sentencing for criminal offences that have an aggravating demonstration of hostility towards members of specified groups. Speech alone is further regulated through the Football Offences and Communications Acts. In addition, police follow-up on and record details of non-crime hate incidents. The result is a complex mess of myriad Acts of Parliament and official police guidance designed to clamp down on speech and behaviour deemed, in the eyes of victims or the perception of observers, to be motivated by hostility.

In the most recent year for which statistics are available, police in England and Wales recorded over 100,000 hate crimes. Only a tiny fraction of these cases hit the headlines. In June 2019, two women, Melania Geymonat and Christine Hannigan, were attacked on a London bus because of their sexuality. Three boys were charged with public order offences and the sentencing judge ruled that they had carried out a hostile act driven by homophobia.[1] Most recently, the

Metropolitan Police have investigated journalist Darren Grimes and historian David Starkey for allegedly stirring up racial hatred in an interview broadcast on *YouTube*. All charges against the pair have since been dropped but, if found guilty, the pair could have faced seven years in prison.

Hate crime is assumed to be on the increase. Statistics obtained by the BBC show there were 6,655 cases of hate crime based on sexual orientation in 2014-2015, and that this rose to 18,465 in 2019-20.[2] However, definitions of hate crime are subjective and depend upon the perception of victims and observers. It is in the interests of activists, campaigning on behalf of a particular identity group, to present hate crime – and therefore the need for protections and additional resources – as increasing.

Attempts to clarify and make the law around hate speech more coherent are currently being undertaken. The Hate Crime and Public Order Bill is currently making its way through the Scottish Parliament. In England and Wales, the Law Commission has published a Consultation Paper setting out proposals for legal changes. In both instances, concerns have been raised about the impact of new legislation on free speech. In this report, we raise far wider concerns about the changing nature of the law and the legal concept of equality.

This report is in two chapters. Chapter one explores the history, current context and impact of hate crime legislation. It draws upon interviews with:

- Dr Carlton Brick, Lecturer in Sociology, University of the West of Scotland, Paisley;

- Harry Miller, former police officer;

- Andrew Tettenborn, Professor of Commercial Law;

- Safe Schools Alliance;

- Kellie-Jay Keen-Minshull (a.k.a Posie Parker), Women's rights campaigner;

- Caroline Farrow;

- Radomir Tylecote, Co-Founder and Director of Research, Free Speech Union.

Chapter two provides a detailed analysis of the Law Commission Consultation Paper on Hate Crime Laws, with a focus on two points in particular: the notion of equality before the law and the challenge to free expression. The consultation's foundations in Critical Legal Theory promote a concept of the law that sees it concerned with promoting social justice. This represents a significant break with the past.

Recommendations

- There should be no extensions to existing hate speech legislation.

- The police should not publish annual records of hate crime statistics that are distinct from, and in addition to, statistics compiled from the Crime Survey for England and Wales.

- Disclosure and Barring Service checks, used to vet people seeking employment with members of vulnerable groups, should not reveal untried accusations of non-crime hate incidents.

- No 'characteristics' should receive special legal protection in a way that violates the principle of equality under the law.

- Curtail the influence of hate crime entrepreneurs. Groups with a vested interest in presenting their members as victims of hate crime should not influence hate crime legislation.

- Hold an inquiry to determine, review and potentially repeal all elements of the law that conflict with freedom of speech, for example: Section 127 of the Communications Act, offences of stirring up hatred under the Public Order Act 1986, and the offence of 'indecent or racialist chanting' under the Football (Offences) Act 1991.

1.

What is a hate crime?

Hate crime is defined as 'any criminal offence which is perceived, by the victim or any other person, to be motivated by hostility or prejudice towards someone based on a personal characteristic.' This common definition was agreed in 2007 by the police, the Crown Prosecution Service (CPS), the Prison Service (now the National Offender Management Service) and other agencies that make up the criminal justice system.[3]

The government's website for people to report hate crime claims 'Crimes committed against someone because of their disability, transgender-identity, race, religion or belief, or sexual orientation are hate crimes and should be reported to the police.'[4] It specifies that hate must be directed at someone on account of their membership of these five particular groups, and not just at them as an individual. These five monitored strands of hate crime are set out in sections 28-32 of the Crime and Disorder Act 1998 and sections 145 and 146 of the Criminal Justice Act 2003. In Scotland, the law likewise currently recognises hate crimes as motivated by prejudice based on race, religion, disability, sexual orientation or transgender identity.

Hate crime can include verbal abuse, intimidation, threats, harassment, assault and bullying targeted at individuals or groups, as well as more general 'stirring up' offences.

Speech is therefore not just a key component of hate crime, but a criminal offence in its own right. As the Law Commission notes: 'The term hate crime is sometimes also used to describe "hate speech" offences, such as offences of stirring up hatred under the Public Order Act 1986, and the offence of "indecent or racialist chanting" under the Football (Offences) Act 1991.'[5] The United Nations defines hate speech as:

> 'any kind of communication in speech, writing or behaviour, that attacks or uses pejorative or discriminatory language with reference to a person or a group based on who they are, in other words, based on their religion, ethnicity, nationality, race, colour, descent, gender or other identity factor. This is often rooted in, and generates intolerance and hatred and, in certain contexts, can be demeaning and divisive.'[6]

There are essentially two components to a hate crime: the criminal offence (for example: assault, theft, murder, damage to property) and the aggravation or motivation for the offence. When a criminal offence is committed, a suspect will be prosecuted and, if found guilty, punished accordingly. If, in addition, the original offence is considered to have been motivated by hostility against the victim on account of their race, religion, sexuality, disability or transgender identity, then the offence is considered to be a hate crime and prosecutors can apply for an uplift in sentence, meaning an increased punishment for those convicted.

The Metropolitan Police note that: 'With hate crime it is "who" the victim is, or "what" the victim appears to be that motivates the offender to commit the crime.'[7] The elements of a person's identity that are singled out for protection under hate crime legislation mirror some (but not all) of the 'protected characteristics' outlined in the Equality Act 2010.[8]

The characteristics of age, sex, marital status, pregnancy and maternity do not warrant additional protections under hate crime legislation. However, there are continual calls to expand the definition of a hate crime, for example, for legislation to encompass misogyny.

Police record not just hate crime but 'hate incidents.' An 'incident' is speech or action perceived to be hostile but that is not, in itself, criminal or associated with a criminal offence. According to the Citizens Advice Bureau, the police and the CPS declare an occurrence to be a hate incident if the victim or anyone else thinks it was motivated by hostility or prejudice but no criminal offence against person or property has taken place.[9] In this way, the motivation of 'hate' becomes separated from a criminal act, and hostile speech, whether verbal or written, directed at an individual or a group, becomes a hate incident requiring police investigation. The police record 'non-crime hate incidents' and although no further legal action may be taken, those accused may still be formally interviewed and warned about their behaviour. The CPS point out that the perpetrator of a hate crime can be a friend, carer or acquaintance who 'exploits their relationship with the victim for financial gain or some other criminal purpose.'[10]

Ascertaining the aggravation or motivation for a crime or non-crime incident is not always straightforward. Clearly, the crime or incident must be committed against a person with 'protected characteristics.' In some cases, spoken or written words may accompany actions and provide insight into the motivation of the perpetrator. However, it is not necessary for the incident to be accompanied by hateful words, it is sufficient for the alleged victim to perceive hate as an aggravating or motivating feature for a hate crime or non-crime incident to be reported. If the target of the incident does not perceive themselves to be a victim of hate then a third party, someone more sensitive to motive, can report hate on their behalf. As the Metropolitan Police spell out: 'Evidence of the hate element is not a requirement. You do not need to personally perceive the incident to be hate related. It would be enough if another person, a witness or even a police officer thought that the incident was hate related.'[11]

When a crime or incident is based upon the victim's perceptions, or the perceptions of a by-stander, the law moves from the terrain of objective facts and into subjective feelings. Far from being challenged, this subjective element is encouraged and reinforced. As director of public prosecutions, Alison Saunders issued updated guidance on dealing with hate crime and urged prosecutors to consider the potential impact of crimes on the wider community as well as the victim.

Non-criminal incidents most frequently take the form of speech and, in particular, speech on social media. This is made clear by London's Metropolitan Police force which includes in its definition of hate crime: 'Someone using offensive language towards you or harassing you because of who you are, or who they think you are, is also a crime. The same goes for someone posting abusive or offensive messages about you online.'[12] In 2017, Saunders announced that online crime would be treated as seriously as offline offences.

Reporting hate crime has been actively encouraged and so, unsurprisingly, recent years have witnessed an increase in the number of recorded incidents and prosecutions for hate crime. Under Saunders, the CPS encouraged 'people to report hate crime incidents through a new social media campaign using the hashtag #HateCrimeMatters.' Saunders said she hoped to 'give people the confidence to come forward and report hate crime, in the knowledge that they will be taken seriously and given the support they need.'[13] The CPS offers links to organisations, other than the police, where people can report their experiences. Reports of hate crime and hate incidents are logged, irrespective of whether or not they are proven to have occurred or whether or not there is a specified victim. In this way, incidents can rise at the same time as criminal convictions fall and all other indicators suggest society is becoming more tolerant towards people from minority communities.

In March 2019, Caroline Farrow, a well-known Catholic commentator, writer and the UK Campaign Director for CitizenGO, was contacted by Surrey Police and threatened with an interview under caution for comments she had made on Twitter. Farrow was told that if she did not attend the interview, she would be arrested. The case was dropped when her accuser withdrew the complaint.

Farrow told me:

'Because I've got a public profile and I've picked up some detractors over the years, people are now reporting me to the police and accusing me of hate crimes all the time, either for things I've said on Twitter or, if they can't find anything I have said, for making anonymous accounts. The first time the police got in touch with me about these accusations was in March 2019.'

'I had been in touch with the police myself, long before this time. I first contacted the police about a blog that was being published online about me. The people behind it were publishing photos of my children, they

---

insulted me, they called me a Catholic cunt, a Catholic bitch, and made obscene sexual suggestions. They published details identifying my childrens' schools and also outlined detailed knowledge of the journey my eldest child makes to and from school every day. Our details and photographs were published on online pornography sites and explicit posts were made in our children's names on teen transgender forums. A malicious online complaint was submitted to the NSPCC – which prompted a same-day welfare check from the police and resulting trauma to the children. I reported this to the police, but they did nothing. Even when these people threatened to come to my house, the police still did nothing. All the while it was getting worse.'

'The police eventually interviewed one man under caution, someone who owned the original site. But then the site moved and the original owner denied having anything to do with it. I was subject to this tsunami of harassment and the police again refused to do anything about it. At one point a police officer asked me, "Are you posting about transgender issues online? You just need to stop that." I felt like a rape victim being told they asked for it because they were wearing a short skirt.'

'What was going on was a hate crime, I was being targeted for my Catholic faith, but the police were not doing anything about it. Worse, they told me that because I was continuing to speak out about what was happening to me, I was asking for it. I told the police I was experiencing a form of cyber bullying that leads people to kill themselves. At this point I was asked for the names and ages of all my children so that social services could be contacted as I had made a suicide threat.'

'Then, in the middle of all of this, in March 2019, the police phoned me up and told me they wanted to speak to me about tweets I had made back in October in which I misgendered Susie Green's daughter. I knew I had been on *Good Morning Britain* with Susie Green [Director of Mermaids, a charity for transgender childen] at that time. But the police wouldn't let me know the full details of what I was being accused of until I came in for an interview. I knew I'd said that she had had her son castrated and that this was child abuse. But I told them this was within my right to free expression. I hadn't bombarded Suzie Green with tweets, I hadn't even copied her into the offending tweet.'

'What really shocked me was the disparity. My family had been threatened, at one point we were receiving takeaways up to 10 times a day, we were receiving notifications of massive orders from companies supplying sex toys and goods to the adult entertainment industry, my children had been targeted and threatened and the police did nothing. Yet I had sent four tweets offering a social commentary on an activist who had chosen to put her story into the public domain and I was being investigated by the police. You get the feeling it's just political. They see this noisy, critical woman who is always complaining and think this is not worth bothering about; whereas as soon as Susie Green complains, a police force comes and knocks on my door. There's been a blog post written musing about whether or not it would be worth disfiguring my children with acid, or whether or not someone is waiting in the bushes "to stab me in the pussy", and no-one does anything. But a few tweets about Susie Green prompts a police investigation.'

'The police told me that I needed to come in for the interview there and then. I said I wanted to get a solicitor but they told me I should use the duty solicitor. I insisted I wanted my own solicitor and they said to me, "if you don't turn up for this interview then a warrant will be issued for your arrest". I told them there was a national conversation about transgender rights and I was just expressing my opinion and I was protected under Article 10 of the European Human Rights Act. She told me I was being charged under the Malicious Communications Act.'

'When I made all this public, it got dropped. All I had been told was that I had been accused of misgendering Susie Green's daughter. Susie Green went on the Victoria Derbyshire Show to say that she'd decided to drop the charges against me because she didn't want me to be the victim. It felt like she was using the police as her personal army because she informed the world she was dropping the charges against me on national television, but the police didn't contact me to let me know this for another two or three days. The police gave me a "mind as you go" warning and told me to watch what I say in the future. Their LGBT liaison officer contacted me to say, "Well, a lot of people have been hurt over the past few days."'

'I'm now being sued, for a second time, by a notorious transgender activist (don't name them) who is attempting to re-open a settled claim against me for comments they are alleging I made over a year ago. I feel constantly exposed. And because of the ongoing harassment, I feel constantly on edge, every time the doorbell rings I jump. I don't trust the police to help me anymore. I try to rationalise things. I like to think I wouldn't be arrested for a false accusation, but I don't have that confidence any more. The police view towards me seems to be that because I put myself out there on social media then I deserve everything I get.'

Legal history

In all parts of the UK, existing hate crime legislation has evolved over time and in a fragmented manner. In recent years, the legal definition of hate crime and non-crime hate incidents has been repeatedly clarified and publicised. As a result, according to the Law Commission's 2020 Consultation on Hate Crime Laws, England and Wales now has 'one of the most comprehensive hate crime reporting and recording systems in the world.'[14] However, in historical context, there is nothing new about prosecuting people for offensive speech.

The earliest restrictions on offensive speech were designed to punish those who challenged or insulted Christianity. They were first introduced during the Medieval Period and not formally abolished until 2008. From 1400, it became a crime under canon law to preach heresy or to own or write heretical books. Bishops had the power to arrest, try and convict offenders, and punishment was often death by burning or hanging. From the 16th century, blasphemy became an offence under common law. This legislation was also used to punish atheists. In 1697, Edinburgh student Thomas Aitkenhead was executed for blasphemy.[15]

In 1867, in the case of *Cowan v Milbourn*, the courts confirmed that Christianity was part of English law. The last person in Britain to be sent to prison for blasphemy was John William Gott on 9 December 1921. He had three previous convictions for blasphemy when he was prosecuted for publishing pamphlets that satirised the biblical story of Jesus entering Jerusalem. Despite outrage at this case, blasphemy laws were still cited in British legal cases many decades later. When the 1977 case *Whitehouse v Lemon* (brought against *Gay News* for publishing James Kirkup's poem *The Love that Dares to Speak its Name*) was appealed in the House of Lords, Lord Scarman said:

> 'I do not subscribe to the view that the common-law offence of blasphemous libel serves no useful purpose in modern law. [...] The offence belongs to a group of criminal offences designed to safeguard the internal tranquility of the kingdom.'[16]

Just as blasphemy laws were being called into question through lack of convictions, other laws began to be created that outlawed offensive speech. The British Race Relations Act 1965 introduced important anti-discrimination protections for minority groups, but Section 6 of this act prohibited 'incitement to racial hatred'. This effectively became the first hate speech offence. The classic example of an incitement to hatred offence is a leaflet or speaker at a meeting of a racist group deliberately stirring up the intended audience with provocative, hate-filled statements about an ethnic minority.[17] Early convictions saw the ringleaders and active members of openly racist organisations charged for use of 'extreme language'.[18] However, the very first person to be prosecuted under this new offence was a black man, and several other black Britons were prosecuted for anti-white hatred, including leaders of the Black Liberation Movement.[19] In 1968, one such leader was sentenced to a year in prison for a speech in which he called white people 'vicious and nasty'.[20]

Two decades on from the Race Relations Act and stirring up hatred on the grounds of race was further prohibited in the offences listed under the Public Order Act 1986. Added to this was 'the stirring up of hatred on grounds of religion or sexual orientation.' Common law offences of blasphemy and blasphemous libel were not abolished in England and Wales until the passing of the Criminal Justice and Immigration Act 2008. For over two decades, speech offensive to religious communities could, potentially, be prosecuted under both blasphemy laws and the Public Order Act. The passing of the 1986 Act demonstrates the tendency of hate speech legislation, once established in principle, to expand in scope.

Section 4 of the Public Order Act 1986 (POA) made it an offence for a person to use 'threatening, abusive or insulting words or behaviour that causes, or is likely to cause, another person harassment, alarm or distress'. We can see how, at the same time as covering a more expansive range of behaviours, offences also became more subjectively defined in relation to the emotional response of the alleged victim. Since 1986, this law has been clarified and revised to include language deemed to incite 'racial and religious hatred', as well as 'hatred on the grounds of sexual orientation' and language that 'encourages terrorism'.

In 1998, Article 10 of the Human Rights Act confirmed that 'everyone has the right to freedom of expression' in the UK, but that this freedom 'may be subject to formalities, conditions, restrictions or penalties as are prescribed by law and are necessary in a democratic society.'[21] Those restrictions may be 'in the interests of national security, territorial integrity or public safety, for the prevention of disorder or crime, for the protection of health or morals, for the protection of the reputation or rights of others, for preventing the disclosure of information received in confidence, or for maintaining the authority and impartiality of the judiciary.' Limiting speech – even for the purposes of protecting 'morals' and safeguarding a person's 'reputation' (in addition to already established libel laws) – is still a curtailment of free expression.

1998 also saw the passing of the Crime and Disorder Act. Sections 28-32 of this act specified strands of hate crime to be monitored by the police and also introduced the concept of 'aggravated offences.' An aggravated offence occurs when a crime is committed by a person who demonstrates, or is motivated by, hostility on the grounds of race or religion. This is the first time that the phrase 'hate crime' is used in relation to a criminal offence.

As the Law Commission acknowledges, one of the most important events driving the development of hate crime legislation in England and Wales over the past three decades has been the murder of Stephen Lawrence in 1993:

> 'Stephen, and his friend Duwayne Brooks were attacked by a group of five or six white youths while waiting for a bus in South East London. Stephen was stabbed at least twice during the attack, severing arteries and penetrating a lung. Duwayne heard one of Stephen's assailants saying "What, what, n****r?" as they approached to attack him. Five suspects had previous links to attacks on members of racial minorities in the area.'[22]

Outcry at the police mishandling of the subsequent murder investigation, including poor treatment of Duwayne Brooks and the Lawrence family, led to the Stephen Lawrence

Inquiry and the publication of the report into the inquiry by Sir William Macpherson in February 1999.

The Macpherson Report concluded that the Metropolitan Police's murder investigation had been 'marred by a combination of professional incompetence, institutional racism and a failure of leadership by senior officers'.[23] The inquiry found that institutional racism extended beyond the Metropolitan Police Service. The drive to tackle racism, and particularly to gather evidence of speech that could 'stir up hatred' in advance of crime being committed, has shaped policy in the subsequent two decades.

Following the murder of Stephen Lawrence, the police placed greater emphasis on recording hate crime. The Association of Chief Police Officers' 2005 hate crime manual required that all hate incidents be recorded, even if they did not meet the legal bar for hate crime. In 2007, the CPS, police and criminal justice agencies began to adopt a broad, operational definition of 'hate crime', primarily for recording purposes. From this time, hate crime became defined as:

> 'any criminal offence which is perceived by the victim or any other person, to be motivated by a hostility or prejudice based on a person's race or perceived race; religion or perceived religion; sexual orientation or perceived sexual orientation; disability or perceived disability and any crime motivated by a hostility or prejudice against a person who is transgender or perceived to be transgender.'

As noted previously, it was also in 2007 that the Public Order Act 1986 was extended to include the stirring up of hatred on the grounds of religion.

The requirement for police to record non-crime hate incidents was reinforced in the government's Hate Crime Action Plan published in 2012, which sought to promote greater consistency in the recording of incidents relating to members of the five protected characteristics. This action plan set out 'core principles' in tackling hate crime, including:

1. Challenging the attitudes that underpin hate crime.

2. Employing early intervention to prevent it escalating.

3. Increasing reporting and access to support by building victim confidence and supporting local partnerships.

4. Improving the operational response to hate crimes by better identifying and managing cases, and dealing effectively with offenders.[24]

Today, many reports of non-crime hate incidents stem from comments found on social media. They are often investigated under Section 127 of the Communications Act 2003 – which made it illegal to send messages via a public electronic communications network that are considered grossly offensive, or of an indecent, obscene or menacing character. Section 127 of the Communications Act has led to some recent high profile police investigations, including the Scottish comedian 'Count Dankula', who was questioned and fined for posting a film of his dog performing a Nazi salute on *YouTube*; Kate Scottow, who was fined for misgendering a transgender activist on Twitter; and Caroline Farrow, who was likewise threatened with a criminal record for offending a transgender activist. The Law Commission has now launched a consultation: Harmful Online Communications: The Criminal Offences.[25]

Also, in 2003, the Criminal Justice Act allowed for enhanced sentencing provisions for people convicted of aggravated offences. Restrictions on free speech were then further tightened by the 2006 Terrorism Act, which criminalises 'encouragement of terrorism'. This includes making statements that glorify terrorist acts.

In 2008, Stonewall and other campaigners successfully persuaded Parliament to make it a crime in England and Wales under the Criminal Justice and Immigration Act to incite hatred against any person based on his or her actual or perceived sexual orientation. Similar legislation had been enacted in Northern Ireland in 2004 under Part 3 of the Public Order (Northern Ireland) Order 1987. The Criminal Justice and Immigration Act 2008 further separated hateful speech from other criminal actions, making speech not an aggravating offence, but an offence in its own right. In 2010, the Public Order Act 1986 was again extended to cover offences involving the stirring up of hatred on the grounds of sexual orientation. In addition to all this legislation, a small number of discrete, specific offences form part of the overall hate crime framework. In particular, the offence of 'indecent or racialist chanting' under the Football (Offences) Act 1991 prohibits engaging or taking part in chanting of an indecent or racialist nature at a designated football match.

The College of Policing (CoP) issued a Hate Crime Manual in 2005 which issued guidance on recording hate incidents. It stressed that 'in a modern democratic and diverse society, protecting all the composite groups of that society in accordance with their needs is vital if the service is to continue to police by consent.' In May 2014, this was updated and published as Hate Crime Operational Guidance. It includes specific information on what can be covered by race hate crime:

> 'Race hate crime can include any group defined by race, colour, nationality or ethnic or national origin, including countries within the UK, and Gypsy or Irish Travellers. It automatically includes a person who is targeted because they are an asylum seeker or refugee as this is intrinsically linked to their ethnicity and origins.'[26]

The CoP's 2014 guidance makes clear that, if effective, the number of people prosecuted for hate crime will increase: 'Targets that see success as reducing hate crime are not appropriate'. Since this time, there have also been a number of awareness-raising campaigns around hate crime, particularly in the wake of the EU referendum. In April 2015, it became mandatory for all forces to return quarterly information on the number of crimes flagged as being committed online (in full or in part)[27] and in 2017, London mayor Sadiq Khan launched the Metropolitan Police's Online Hate Crime Hub.[28]

In a foreword to the 2014 update, the point is made that:

'Hate crimes are far more prevalent than official statistics suggest. [...] Hate crimes can have a greater emotional impact on the victim than comparable non-hate crimes, and can cause increased levels of fear and anxiety that can also permeate through wider communities. This is precisely why all victims should not be treated the same. Rather, they should receive a service from the police that is appropriate to their needs.'

The foreword continues by quoting the Macpherson Report into the murder of Stephen Lawrence: 'The police service must: ...deliver a service which recognises the different experiences, perceptions and needs of a diverse society.'[29]

In 2019, the College of Policing launched a review of its Hate Crime Operational Guidance, and in October 2020 issued the Authorised Professional Practice Guidance on Hate Crime. This review takes account of 'the findings from a High Court ruling in February 2020 when a claim that the College's previous hate crime operational guidance for police was unlawful was rejected.'[30] The new guidance has 'clear advice for officers and staff on the steps they should take when responding to non-crime hate incidents, including proportionate responses to take depending on the nature of the report and strategies to manage contact with all parties involved.' It remains the case that a record of someone having been questioned in relation to a non-crime hate incident may show up if they undergo an enhanced Disclosure and Barring Service (DBS) check in order to work or volunteer with groups considered vulnerable.

Currently, a Hate Crime and Public Order (Scotland) Bill is making its way through the Scottish Parliament.[31] The aim is that new legislation 'will provide greater clarity, transparency and consistency' by bringing 'most of Scotland's hate crime legislation into one statute'.[32] If enacted, the Scottish bill will abolish the common law offence of blasphemy but, at the same time, make provision about the aggravation of offences by prejudice and offences relating to stirring up hatred against a group of persons. This effectively recriminalises blasphemy, and those found guilty could be jailed for up to seven years. Offences of 'stirring up hatred' in the bill include behaving in a threatening, abusive or insulting manner, or sending material of this kind to another person. The bill goes so far as to outlaw the 'possession' of 'inflammatory material [...] with a view to communicating [it] to another person'.

In England and Wales, the Law Commission has recently launched a consultation proposing changes to hate crime laws. The starting point is that criminal prohibitions on hate speech and hate crime are 'well established in the law of England and Wales, and the trend in recent years has broadly been to expand the scope of these protections to additional characteristic groups.'[33]

Protected characteristics

As we see from the above discussion, there is no overarching UK-wide legislation against hate speech. The Law

Commission notes: 'The law in England and Wales currently offers enhanced criminal protection, in different forms, to individuals and groups on the basis of race, religion, disability, sexual orientation and transgender identity.' In this way, over the past decade, changes to the law around offensive speech – and the way that existing laws are interpreted – have increasingly mirrored the Equality Act 2010, which offers additional legal safeguards to individuals with 'protected characteristics'. Under the Equality Act, 'It is against the law to discriminate against someone because of a protected characteristic.'[34] Discrimination, in this context, can be direct or indirect and include harassment and victimisation.

The Equality Act 2010 identifies nine protected characteristics:

1. age;

2. disability;

3. gender reassignment;

4. marriage and civil partnership;

5. pregnancy and maternity;

6. race;

7. religion or belief;

8. sex;

9. sexual orientation.[35]

For each protected characteristic, the act specifies the conditions in which direct or indirect discrimination, harassment or victimisation can be said to have occurred. It also outlines circumstances in which differential treatment may be legal, for example, a theatre company looking to hire a young boy to play a particular role or in cases where a business is looking to take positive action to promote members of under-represented groups. The act aims to provide a legal framework for protecting the rights of individuals and advancing equality of opportunity for all. The Equality and Human Rights Commission describes it as 'a discrimination law which protects individuals from unfair treatment and promotes a fair and more equal society.'[36]

The Equality Act 2010 was one of the last measures enacted by the Labour government before it lost office in May 2010. It came about after years of campaigning by activists and human rights organisations. Over several decades, the law gradually began to recognise the rights of a wider range of disadvantaged groups. At the same time, the legally-recognised understanding of equality shifted from 'formal' to 'substantive' as it was increasingly accepted that achieving equality required a shift from treating people identically to accommodating differences. The Equality Act was brought into operation by the subsequent Conservative-Liberal Democrat Coalition government. It draws together many separate pieces of legislation, including, most notably:

- Equal Pay Act 1970;
- Sex Discrimination Act 1975;
- Race Relations Act 1976;
- Disability Discrimination Act 1995;
- Employment Equality (Religion or Belief) Regulations 2003;
- Employment Equality (Sexual Orientation) Regulations 2003;
- Employment Equality (Age) Regulations 2006;
- Equality Act 2006, Part 2;
- Equality Act (Sexual Orientation) Regulations 2007.

The Sex Discrimination Act (1975) first introduced the concept of indirect discrimination: the idea that a practice, policy or rule can apply to everyone in the same way, but in so doing has a worse effect on some people than others. It gave legal permission for positive discrimination: treating people differently in order to bring about equality. In 1989, the Fair Employment (Northern Ireland) Act imposed positive duties to achieve fair participation of the Catholic and Protestant communities on certain employers. In 1998 this was reformed to impose positive duties on public bodies to have due regard to the need to promote equality of opportunity, not only between Protestant and Catholic communities, but also in respect of age, disability, race, religion, sex, marital status, and sexual orientation. Public bodies had to mainstream equality into all of their functions.

This approach was adopted in Britain from 2000, in respect of race equality, following the inquiry into the death of Stephen Lawrence – which accused the Metropolitan Police of institutional racism. The subsequent Cambridge Review proposed that there should be a single Equality Act adopting a unitary or integrated approach covering all protected characteristics; this became the Equality Act 2010.[37]

As previously indicated, hate crime legislation has not been formally brought together in a unifying Act of Parliament in the same way as equalities legislation. However, both the CPS and the government's website for reporting hate crime define offenses in the same way, drawing upon the list of characteristics presented in the Equality Act. When hate crime is defined as crime motivated by '"who" the victim is, or "what" the victim appears to be' then it readily becomes attached to groups already legally designated as vulnerable to discrimination, harassment and victimisation. Equalities and hate crime legislation have become intrinsically linked.

Another common suggestion is that the characteristics protected by hate crime laws should be consistent with those protected in anti-discrimination law. As noted, the Equality Act 2010 recognises nine protected characteristics. These include the five hate crime characteristics specified in the Criminal Justice Act 2003. The category of 'religion or belief' is significantly broader than its equivalent in hate crime law because it includes non-religious 'belief'. The term 'gender reassignment' is used rather than 'transgender identity'. The Equality Act also provides protection against discrimination on the basis of sex, age, marriage or civil partnership status, and being pregnant or on maternity leave.

The Hate Crime and Public Order (Scotland) Bill and the Law Commission's Consultation on Hate Crime Laws both consider the case for closer alignment between hate crime and equalities legislation. Professor Andrew Tettenborn explains:

'The Equality Act is only concerned with the civil liability for discrimination, it brought in this list of protected characteristics which obviously includes sex. But what they are currently trying to do in Scotland and what is being proposed for England is to get the structure of this, the civil law rules on discrimination, carried over into the criminal law so that anyone who falls under the protected characteristics ought to be given legal protection if anyone offends them. This is an equality of illiberalism.'[38]

There are clear similarities between equalities and hate crime legislation: both offer protection to members of disadvantaged groups. However, each serves a different purpose – equality laws are primarily designed to prevent discrimination in civil law contexts such as employment, education, health care and other forms of service provision. Hate crime, by contrast, is designed for the criminal law, where the role of the state is greater and the implications for offenders more severe. The Law Commission's Consultation on hate crime legislation concludes: 'Ultimately, while we consider many useful comparisons can be drawn between equality law and hate crime law, we are concerned that the differences between the civil and criminal contexts are too great to justify the adoption of this approach.'[39]

Prosecutions and investigations

According to Home Office statistics, in 2018/19 police in England and Wales recorded 103,379 hate crimes. This represented an increase of 10 per cent on the previous year; in 2017/18, 94,121 offences were recorded. In turn, the 2017/18 figure was up 17 per cent on 2016/17. This continual upward trend means that the number of hate crimes recorded by the police has more than doubled since 2012/13 (from 42,255 to 103,379 offences).[40] There were increases in all five centrally monitored strands, although around three-quarters of all recorded offences (76 per cent; 78,991) were race hate crimes.

The Law Commission notes that:

'Compared with other jurisdictions, the extent to which hate crime is being reported and prosecuted in England and Wales is notable. For example, in Canada, which has a population of approximately 37 million, the number of hate crimes reported to police in 2018 was 1,798. In England and Wales, which has a population of nearly 59 million (about 50% larger), the police recorded hate crime figure was 94,098. As a proportion of the population, this was around 35 times the Canadian figure. While it is possible that the incidence of hate crime is indeed lower in Canada than in the United Kingdom, it is doubtful that this comes close to accounting for such a huge disparity. A more likely explanation is the differing legal tests for hate crime in these jurisdictions. The "demonstration of hostility" approach in the jurisdictions of the United Kingdom allows for a significantly broader array of conduct to be treated as hate crime.'

The Home Office acknowledges that 'increases in hate crime over the last five years have been mainly driven by improvements in crime recording by the police'.[41] As previously noted, the expansive and subjective nature of hate crime combined with well publicised campaigns to encourage not just victims, but those who perceive offence on behalf of others, to come forward may lead to large increases in recorded crimes without any actual change in people's behaviour. The more police pro-actively seek hate crimes to record, the more likely they are to find what they are looking for.

The women's rights campaigner Kellie-Jay Keen-Minshull (who campaigns under the name Posie Parker) was interviewed by two separate police forces after being accused of committing a hate crime by Susie Green, the director of Mermaids, a charity supporting transgender children.[42]

Keen-Minshull described her experience:

'I put up a billboard with the definition of the word woman on it and this prompted some run-ins with a particular individual on social media. The next thing I knew, I got text messages from the police. They got my details from Twitter. But I ignored it because I thought it was a joke.'

'Eventually I thought I'd better phone them back to check and the police officer I spoke to said he was following up a complaint from Susie Green, the head of Mermaids. He was trying to be very friendly, implying

---

he was on my side and I said to him, 'People tweet about Trump all the time and Susie Green is a public figure so surely it's fair game to comment on what she's up to.' It was such a friendly chat; we were just laughing about it. But I mentioned it to some friends and they put me in touch with a solicitor. And then four weeks later when I was called back by the police and they knew I had a solicitor and their whole manner towards me just changed completely.'

'Suddenly, the police officer wasn't being friendly any more. He said, "If you try and leave the country, we'll arrest you. If you're pulled over by the police, we'll arrest you. We'll come to your house and arrest you in front of your children. We'll put you in the cells. Then I'll come down from Yorkshire, which, as you know, will take a long time." He was implying that I'd be sitting in the cells all that time. So, my solicitor came with me, we'd prepared a statement which was read out and then they asked me questions. They said things like: "You do know that sex reassignment surgery doesn't include castration?" I mean, what do they think happens?'

'I prepared myself. I didn't smile. I just said, "No comment." This was all on the basis of six tweets. We know this is happening up and down the country and people don't say anything because they think they are wrong but I know I am right. I was hoping it would go to court. I knew I was right and it takes people like me to stand up to it.'

'It went to the CPS and they sent it back. Susie Green got very annoyed about this and tried to get it appealed but she didn't succeed. I then got interviewed under caution again because I made a video which had a picture of Susie Green in the background. I had it framed in my office. And, as a joke, I pointed to it and said, "Children's champion, Susie Green." I said that transitioning children is abuse and I would say this in a court of law, so bring it on. And that, apparently, is a threat. So those two things got me another interview. This time the policewoman was trying to be polite but I just looked away. It's like a game. I wanted to appear powerful.'

'The second time around, I found out that the police had dropped the charges against me from Twitter. I read about it from someone I follow. The first time they phoned me they said, "We've got some good news for you. The CPS have decided not to charge you." He expected me to be grateful but I said, "No. You've wasted my time, you've wasted taxpayers' money. You should be ashamed of yourself." The state is working for a tiny portion of hardcore activists.'

The Home Office explains some of the recent increase in police recorded statistics as resulting from 'spikes in hate crime following certain events such as the EU Referendum and the terrorist attacks in 2017.'[43] However, the tendency for greater awareness and increased publicity to lead to increased reporting means there is no way of knowing whether such spikes represent a genuine increase in hate-fuelled behaviour or a greater sensitivity to offence and an increased propensity to report offenders. Nonetheless, this ambiguity does not prevent hate crime statistics becoming a tool for activists to further their cause.

Year-on-year increases in hate incidents have been used to argue that hatred and bigotry are rife in post-Brexit Britain. For example, Eryl Jones, from the charity *Show Racism the Red Card*, told the BBC in 2019, 'Incidents of racism have gone up throughout the UK as well as in Wales since the campaign to leave the EU. It's fairly obvious that Brexit has been a major influence. The feeling is that a lot of people believe they have the right to express their racist feelings or to show hatred.' In the same article, Eadyth Crawford, a singer and music tutor from Merthyr Tydfil, is reported as saying that racist opinions have always existed but the Brexit vote has allowed them to be aired more freely: 'Because Brexit appeals to these kinds of people, it's brought them out of the shadows,' she said.[44] That such views are sought and reported uncritically suggests they confirm the assumptions of the BBC journalists.

A separate set of hate crime statistics is compiled from the Crime Survey for England and Wales (CSEW), a face-to-face victimisation survey. This is a general household population survey and, as such, the Home Office maintains that 'the number of hate crime incidents and victims estimated in a single survey year is too unreliable to report on.'[45] Why police recorded hate crime in any one year is a significantly more reliable measure is not explained. The CSEW combines three annual datasets in order to provide a larger sample size and, arguably, produce statistically more robust estimates.

The most recently published CSEW data is from 2017/18. It suggests that there were around 184,000 incidents of hate crime a year. This is substantially higher than the police recorded hate crime statistics. This is to be expected: for many and varied reasons, not all victims of a crime report their experiences to the police. Based on the 2015/16 to 2017/18 CSEW, overall 53 per cent of hate crime incidents came to the attention of the police. Furthermore, the nature of hate crime means that some victims may not even be aware that a crime had been committed against them until their experiences are interpreted by a researcher. Nonetheless, the CSEW statistics suggest that hate crime represents roughly three per cent of all crime (6,096,000 incidents), which does bring it in line with a similar level in the police recorded crime series (2 per cent).[46]

It is worth noting that whereas police statistics show year-on-year increases in recorded hate crimes, CSEW data suggests the opposite, that the longer-term trend is for a reduction in the number of hate crime incidents. The CSEW shows a statistically significant fall in the number of hate crime incidents, from 307,000 in the combined 2007-2009 data to 184,000 2015-2018. This represents a fall of 40 per cent in the decade between 2007/08 and 2017/18. This is in line with a similar percentage fall (39 per cent) in crime overall in the same time period; in other words, rates of hate crime have fallen as other crimes have also fallen.[47] Interestingly, the majority of press coverage concerning hate crime focuses on police statistics showing a large increase, rather than on CSEW data showing a substantial decline. This suggests that hate crime statistics have become unhelpfully politicised.

As with police recorded hate crime, CSEW data shows that the most commonly perceived motivation for committing a hate crime was the offender's attitude to the victim's race. The monitored strand least commonly perceived as an offender's motivation for committing a crime was the victim's gender-identity (the number of CSEW respondents who were victims of this type of hate crime was too low to provide a robust estimate).[48] Police statistics likewise show that the lowest number of reported hate crimes were committed against people based upon their perceived gender identity (2,333 reported incidents). However, this strand of hate crime also showed the sharpest increase (up 37 per cent on the previous year). Again, we cannot be certain whether this represents an increase in incidents or greater awareness leading to an increased propensity for reporting.

According to Home Office data, in 2018/19, just 11 per cent of police recorded hate crime offences were dealt with by a charge or summons. The most frequent outcome recorded for violent offences (32 per cent) was 'evidential difficulties as the victim does not support action.'[49] In other words, the victim either did not concur that hate had been an aggravating factor in the crime committed against them or did not wish to pursue a complaint. In 2018/19, the CPS reported that the number of hate crime prosecutions completed decreased from 14,151 in 2017/18 to 12,828 in 2018/19; a fall of 9.3 per cent. This real terms decrease in prosecutions comes against a large increase in recorded hate crimes.

In 2018/19 the conviction rate for hate crime offences remained consistent with the previous year at 84.3 per cent, and the proportion of cases involving a guilty plea increased slightly from 75.4 per cent in 2017/18 to 76.1 per cent. The proportion of cases resulting in a conviction with an announced and recorded sentence uplift was 73.6 per cent in 2018/19, an increase of 6.5 per cent on the previous year. The CPS Annual Report 2018/19 shows that the number of hate crime cases sent to the CPS by the police fell by 16.7 per cent from 12,901 in 2017/18 to 10,749 in 2018/19. In its 2018/19 annual Hate Crime Report, the CPS notes, with concern, 'the growing gap between the number of hate crimes reported to the police and the number of cases being sent by the police to the CPS for prosecution.'[50] Plans are set out as to how this situation can be ameliorated with police officers encouraged to be more proactive in forwarding incidents to the CPS.

Expansive concept

Over a period of several decades, the concept of hate crime has expanded. Whereas early legislation sought to protect people from violence and harassment on the basis of their race or religion; today, a wider range of characteristics are protected and speech or behaviour perceived either by the victim or by a witness to be driven by hate, irrespective of motive, is now criminalised.

In practice, this means that the law has shifted from prosecuting individuals who clearly and deliberately target a specific victim, or victims, for abuse on account of their race or religion, to prosecuting people whose speech or behaviour, while having no deliberate motive or particular victim, causes general offence by-proxy. Running alongside this expansion of the law is a drive to record more reported incidents and increase the number of investigations, prosecutions and convictions.

In March 2012, the government published *Challenge it, Report it, Stop it: The Government's Plan to Tackle Hate Crime*.[51] Lynne Featherstone MP, then Minister for Equality, explained: 'This Action Plan [...] brings together the work of a wide range of Departments and agencies to: prevent hate crime happening in the first place; increase reporting and victims' access to support; and improve the operational response to hate crimes.' The action plan begins by acknowledging that the inquiry into the death of Stephen Lawrence and the subsequent Macpherson Report had been a catalyst for change, 'not just in the way the police and criminal justice system deal with racially-motivated crimes, but in the recognition of hate crimes more broadly.' It then sets out the Coalition Government's strategy for preventing hate crime by:

- Challenging the attitudes that underpin it, and early intervention to prevent it escalating;

- Increasing reporting and access to support by building victim confidence and supporting local partnerships;

- Improving the operational response to hate crimes by better identifying and managing cases, and dealing effectively with offenders.

Challenge It, Report It, Stop It indicates that regions of the UK are free 'to include other strands in addition to the monitored five when developing their approach to hate crime. For example, some areas have included age or gender in their response to hate crime, to reflect the concerns of local citizens or in response to trends in local crime.'

In 2013, the Law Commission published a consultation paper, *Hate Crime: The Case for Extending the Existing Offences*.[52] This paper, arising out of a cross-departmental government initiative on hate crime, considered the case for extending aggravated offences under the Crime and Disorder Act 1998 and stirring up hatred offences under the Public Order Act 1986. The aim (in part now realised) was to create offences involving hostility on the grounds of disability, sexual orientation and transgender identity. Hate crime legislation expands to keep up with social and political shifts in thinking.

Hate speech legislation also expands to keep pace with technological advances. The Online Harms White Paper was published in 2020 following a consultation to review the details of the communications offences in section 1 of the Malicious Communications Act 1988 and section 127 of the Communications Act 2003. The consultation noted 'significant gaps where the law does not adequately cover genuinely harmful communications (such as "cyber-flashing" or "pile-on harassment").'[53] It offers proposals 'to improve the protection afforded to victims by the criminal law, while at the same time providing better safeguards for freedom of expression.'

The White Paper 'puts forward ambitious plans for a new system of accountability and oversight for tech companies, moving far beyond self-regulation. A new regulatory framework for online safety will make clear companies' responsibilities to keep UK users, particularly children, safer online with the most robust action to counter illegal content and activity.' It proposes 'an independent regulator,' for the internet, 'which will set clear safety standards, backed up by reporting requirements and effective enforcement powers.' The legislation will constitute, 'the first attempt globally to address a comprehensive spectrum of online harms in a single and coherent way.'[54]

The Law Commission notes that seven per cent of those prosecuted under 'communications offences' are also recorded as having committed a hate crime. It describes online abuse as 'a large and growing concern amongst groups who experience hate crime and hate speech.'[55]

Radomir Tylecote, research director at the Free Speech Union, explained the impact the Online Harms Bill will have on free speech:

'The Online Harms Bill tries to tackle many different problems with one mass piece of legislation. There are clearly some genuine online harms. For example, the government is right to look at the distribution of images of child abuse and the use of the internet by terrorists. But most of these things are criminal anyway and the government can further address these problems, but outside a bill that does many other things including censoring free speech.'

'Those proposing this legislation see it as a means of increasing tolerance and reducing hate, but it will have the opposite effect. It's an autocratic approach to free speech. It reveals that the people who write this legislation have lost faith in the marketplace of ideas. They believe that they, or people like them, are better placed to judge facts and ascertain the truth, and that they are best placed to suppress bad ideas.'

'This proposed legislation treats the internet as if it is a retail forum with various product lines that need regulation to make them safe. But trying to regulate the internet in this way, with one white paper, is ridiculous. It's like trying to regulate the entirety of human debate. It's like trying to regulate the world. When we do this, we get all kinds of side effects.

'There's certainly a discussion to be had about bullying and intimidation online. But it is impossible to regulate bullying and intimidation without de facto banning speech. Online companies will be expected to remove huge swathes of what is just ordinary human conversation. Banning intimidation is likely to be interpreted as a prohibition on insulting the government and offensive political commentary. These things can easily feel intimidatory to some and, in a sense, they are: they are often cases of aggressive debate designed to change people's minds. Political aggression – in the sense of people getting angry and insulting each other – is an inevitable part of democratic debate – but it will be classed as intimidation and be outlawed. In the end, large parts of this legislation will fail, but if it fails over ten years then we have a highly regulated internet for a decade.'

'Some groups now have a vested interest in finding hate. There are academics who have become authorities on hate crime and now have a career interest in getting the government to measure and tackle "hate speech". It becomes almost a sock puppet phenomenon: the state pays academics through state-subsidised research councils to tell it to expand its power. There is also a culturally authoritarian world view that now exists among the bureaucratic elite. They regard their role as managing the populace, managing and improving our mental well-being and modifying our behaviour for the better.'

'One idea driving the Online Harms Bill is concern that the public is very gullible and needs authoritative fact-checked news. The argument is that this will help protect them from Russian disinformation, for example, but this is very similar to the arguments made by the Russian and Chinese governments. There is a great irony here: the people writing this legislation think it is needed because people are gullible to conspiracy theories, but they themselves are actually driven by conspiratorial thinking. There is the Carole Cadwalladr view that electoral outcomes are not legitimate and come from people being manipulated online. But there is no evidence for these claims. When bureaucrats believe in conspiracy theories, they demonstrate they are no better than the people they want to manage.'

'Civil society has the capacity to deal with conspiracy

theories. People in authoritarian societies are far more likely to believe in conspiracy theories because they know that information is managed and that it's unreliable. The state, in trying to create fact-checked news, creates an environment in which conspiracy theories will flourish. We are creating the authoritarian environment that will be a hotbed of conspiracy theories.'

'There are child protection charities who quite rightly want more to be done about online paedophilia and images of child abuse. They've pushed for parts of the Online Harms Bill, but their entirely understandable concerns have been manipulated by other people. Their concerns have been put into a bill that covers a great many other issues – and, in my view, doesn't actually cover their concerns very well. There are much better ways to deal with online child abuse and terrorist activity – for example, more resources for policing in these areas and harsher sentences for those found guilty – this is a deterrent.'

'The Online Harms Bill puts a duty of care on online companies and makes them responsible for what happens to users or what users do to each other after viewing material on their site – this could be potentially infinite. Much of this is driven by concern that children might hurt themselves or each other after seeing images of self-harm online. That is an understandable concern. But where are the definitions? According to current plans, children will not be protected but adults will be infantilised. These harms existed before the internet – the internet also acts as a mirror to our society and reflects all the problems we have. But the internet can also provide a means for dealing with some of these problems. In attempting to deal with the online depiction of self-harm we have to be careful that we don't stop the teenager who googles: "How can I stop my sister from self-harming?". If all the material that can help children is removed from the internet then we haven't solved the problem, we've just buried it.'

Hate crime entrepreneurs

Hate Crime: The Case for Extending the Existing Offences drew upon available statistical data as well as 'preliminary fact-finding discussions with several organisations with relevant expertise.'[56] The list of organisations consulted includes those that support and campaign on behalf of people with disabilities, transgender people, and the lesbian, gay and bisexual community. They include:

- Association of Chief Police Officers;
- CPS;
- Disability Hate Crime Network;
- Disability Rights UK;
- Equality and Diversity Forum;
- Equality and Human Rights Commission;
- GALOP;
- Gender Trust;
- GIRES;
- Government Equalities Office;

- Her Majesty's Crown Prosecution Service Inspectorate;

- Home Office;

- Mencap;

- Ministry of Justice;

- National Aids Trust;

- National Autistic Society;

- National Offender Management Service;

- Press for Change;

- Sentencing Council;

- Stonewall;

- StopHate UK;

- Trans Media Watch;

- Victims' Services Alliance;

- Victim Support.

The demand for ever broader definitions of hate crime and for additional groups to be protected has been driven by these identity-based campaigners and activist groups with influence within politics, the law and policing. Some of these organisations offer hate crime reporting services and assist those affected by hate crime to deal effectively with the police and provide the information necessary for further investigation and prosecution. All have a vested interest in expanding definitions of hate crime to encompass the groups they represent and, arguably, have a vested interest in seeing increased reporting of hate crimes committed as a basis for their own future fundraising. For this reason, these organisations are best thought of as 'hate crime entrepreneurs'.

Given the influence of hate crime entrepreneurs, it is hardly surprising that *Hate Crime: The Case for Extending the Existing Offences*, 'leads us to offer provisional proposals for new aggravated offences.'[57] The parameters and analysis of the consultation, along with the groups consulted, determine the nature and scope of likely responses.

A further government report was published in July 2016, *Action Against Hate: the UK Government's Plan to Tackle Hate Crime*.[58] Amber Rudd, then Home Secretary, sets out how 'Together, the Home Office, the Department for Communities and Local Government, and the Ministry of Justice are acting to prevent hate crime, support victims, and prosecute the perpetrators.' Although released only one month after the UK's referendum on EU membership, the report was quick to note: 'In the days after the EU referendum, some European nationals were the targets of abuse, and representatives of other ethnic communities have reported anxiety about a climate of increased hostility towards people identified as foreigners.' An enhanced role for the CoP is identified:

> 'we have also established joint training between the police and Crown Prosecution staff to improve the way the police identify and investigate hate crime. Alongside this training, the College of Policing, as the professional body for policing, has published a national strategy and operational guidance in this area to ensure that policing deals with hate crime effectively.'

The role of hate crime entrepreneurs in this 2016 *Plan to Tackle Hate Crime* is made clear:

> 'The actions set out in this document have been developed through discussions with those communities most affected by hate crime. It is those communities and the organisations

that represent them that often respond to hate crime at the local level, working to tackle hate crime in their area and provide support to victims. This Action Plan represents a partnership between the Government, the criminal justice agencies (the Police Service, the CPS, the courts and the National Offender Management Service) and community groups representing those affected by hate crime. It has been developed with the support of the Independent Advisory Group on hate crime.'[59]

Drawing upon evidence from organisations that represent communities affected by hate crime in compiling guidance for tackling hate crime raises significant issues. Such organisations lobby for better protections for their members. In order to secure these protections, they are incentivised to increase the reporting of hate crimes committed against members of their particular identity group. This lends itself to ever looser definitions of hate crime and ever more expansive cohorts of victims. Furthermore, many groups that lobby on behalf of particular communities receive government funding for their work. For example, *Challenge It, Report It, Stop It* reports on plans to support a range of groups such as the Jewish Museum, Show Racism the Red Card, Searchlight Educational Trust and Faith Matters' Measuring Anti-Muslim Attacks (MAMA) project. As a result, these groups are effectively paid by the government to tell government ministers (via civil servants) what they want to hear.

A similar group of 'hate crime entrepreneurs' contributed to the 2020 Law Commission Consultation on Hate Crime. The authors explain:

'We began this review in March 2019, publishing a brief background paper, and hosting an academic conference at Oxford Brookes University. Throughout the remainder of

2019 we conducted several pre-consultation events across England and Wales. This included meetings with legal and academic experts, police and the Crown Prosecution Service ('CPS'), charities and civil society groups, and numerous individuals with an interest in hate crime laws. With the assistance of the CPS, Citizens UK, HEAR (a London-based equality network) and Dimensions UK (a Learning Disability charity), we also had the opportunity to speak directly with many victims of hate crime, who bravely shared their stories with us. We were humbled by these experiences, and we are extremely grateful for these important contributions.'

As the consultation paper makes clear, these hate crime entrepreneurs, along with academics, play a significant role in determining the assumptions and theoretical underpinnings for the Law Commission's analysis. The role and influence of contributors is evident in the paper's acknowledgement that 'every submission to the inquiry containing data about local or national trends had agreed that: the situation is getting worse and that, due to large numbers of hate crimes not being reported to third-party services or the police, the true profile of hate crime in the UK is akin to an iceberg, with the majority hidden from view.'[60]

Non-crime hate incidents

One unintended consequence of the expansion of hate crime legislation was the police investigation into a speech given by then Home Secretary, Amber Rudd, at the Conservative Party conference in October 2016. In her speech, Rudd said that she wanted to make it harder for British companies to employ migrants and to ensure foreign workers 'were not taking jobs British workers could do'.[61] Rudd did not use racial slurs or name specific individuals. She expressed a legitimate political view that, whether we agree with it or not, echoes similar remarks made previously by politicians from all parties. Joshua Silver, a physics professor at Oxford University, is not a migrant and he was not present when Rudd made her speech. Indeed, he was not at the Conservative Party conference at all. Silver was, however, sufficiently alarmed by the media coverage of Rudd's speech that he reported the Home Secretary to the police. 'I felt politicians have been using hate speech to turn Britons against foreigners, and I thought that is probably not lawful,' he told *The Times* newspaper.

National police reporting rules endorsed by Rudd herself require all complaints of hate crime incidents to be recorded 'regardless of whether or not those making the complaint are the victim and irrespective of whether or not there is any evidence to identify the hate crime incident'. This policy of blanket recording of all complaints was drawn up by the CoP in 2014, with the justification that increased reporting would help police to tackle hate crime more effectively.[62]

Harry Miller, a former police officer from Humberside who now leads the campaign group Fair Cop, was investigated by the police following a complaint made against him over a poem he posted on Twitter and several other tweets that intervened in the ongoing debate about gender identity, often in a humorous way. For example, one of Miller's tweets read: 'I was assigned mammal at birth, but my orientation is fish. Don't mis-species me.' Following complaints, a 'cohesion officer' from Humberside Police telephoned Miller in January 2019 and told him that, while his tweets had not broken any laws, he should not engage in political debate on Twitter 'because some people don't like it'.

Although no crime was committed, Miller was recorded as having committed a hate incident. In Miller's words:

'My retweeting of a gender critical verse had apparently so enraged someone from "down south" that they felt it their civil duty to act as Offended-in-Chief on behalf of my employees "up north." Not that anyone from my firm of around 90 staff had complained, of course, but again… that's beside the point. PC Gul rang my work, spoke to my MD, then spent 32 minutes lecturing me on hurt feelings and in-vitro body parts accidentally growing from a lady brain as I sat with my shopping at Tesco. Sarcasm, satire and talk of synthetic breasts was sufficient to prompt the most urgent of police intervention. That PC Gul didn't appear in Tesco car park with his blues and twos blaring, I suppose, is a small mercy.'[63]

Miller sued Humberside Police. His barrister, Ian Wise QC, argued the force's response had sought to 'dissuade him from expressing himself on such issues in the future' and had a 'substantial chilling effect' on his right to free speech. In February 2020 the High Court ruled that the force's response to Miller's tweets had been unlawful and a 'disproportionate interference' with his right to freedom of expression. Mr Justice Julian Knowles said the effect of police turning up at Mr Miller's place of work 'because of his political opinions must not be underestimated'. He added: 'To do so would be to undervalue a cardinal democratic freedom. In this country we have never had a Cheka, a Gestapo or a Stasi. We have never lived in an Orwellian society.'[64]

I spoke with Harry Miller about the police recording of hate incidents and his own experience of the law in this area:

'It emerged in the Stephen Lawrence inquiry that the police had intelligence of white men sitting around saying they would like to kill a black man. But because this happened in private and it didn't contravene the Public Order Act, there was no actual plotting and so the intelligence was unusable. Macpherson decided that such intelligence would have been useful for the police to capture, particularly in light of the murder of Stephen Lawrence. There was a deliberate move to lower the bar for intelligence purposes so the police could capture that which falls below the level of criminality but which nevertheless might be of interest to future investigations.'

'So, this is where the category of hate incident comes from. A hate incident falls short of a crime but is of interest to the police and helps them gain a picture of what's going on and prevent crime from occurring. This is all very noble. But problems arise when we start looking at definitions. There is no definition of hate. According to the College of Policing guidance, hate can be just disliking someone. But disliking someone shouldn't be a crime. It should be animosity, which, if left unchecked, is likely to tip over into some form of criminal action. On top of this, hatred is then understood as anything a person perceives as hatred. So, it's not even a loose definition of ill will. It's a perception of ill will. It just needs anyone, perhaps a police officer, to believe there was a motive of hate directed at a person who falls under one of the five monitored strands.'

'Hate crime and hate incidents are both recorded on a sheet called a crime report. I'm now down as a "suspect" and the language is one of "offence", and this is still the case even after the judge in my court case ruled that there was no hate, no harassment, and no possibility of this escalating to become a crime. Nevertheless, my case remains a hate incident statistic at both local and national level. Whether or not this would show up should I require a DBS check is entirely at the whim of the chief constable. It's an arbitrary decision. But British law should not work with this degree of arbitrariness.'

'Unfortunately, by challenging and then beating Humberside Police at the High Court, we have inadvertently made some things worse. Prior to Miller vs Humberside Police, if the police were notified of a hate incident then there was a high degree of likelihood that they would contact the suspect and ask them what they were doing and so the suspect would, at very least, be aware that there had been a complaint made against them. Since Miller has gone through, the police are now reluctant to approach suspects because Humberside Police were told by the High Court judge that, in approaching me, they had behaved like the Gestapo and the Stasi.'

'But the High Court also ruled that the simple act of recording an incident was legal. So now, the police are recording hate incidents but not letting the people accused know. The first thing you will know about it might be when you don't get a job you applied for.'

'We thought we would either win or lose at the High Court. What we didn't imagine was that we would beat Humberside but, at the same time, the court would declare that the recording was legal. The College of Policing covered the Humberside defence and said that Humberside followed the national guidance to the letter. So now we're in a situation where the guidance and the recording are legal, but following the guidance is illegal. We could not possibly have anticipated this. The College of Policing is still defending Humberside. They have not altered their guidance – they don't want to have to admit there is anything wrong with it.'

'One problem today is that there's the emergence of an officer class within the police. These are people who have been on all the diversity training programmes. But the upshot is they are no longer clear about the difference between guidance and the law. Some police forces have now signed up to the Stonewall champion scheme and have entirely bought into Stonewall's notion of transphobia. But not all forces have. I live on the border of Lincolnshire and Humberside; Lincolnshire is not part of the Stonewall champion scheme but Humberside is.'

'In 2003 the police oath changed from upholding the law and keeping the peace to upholding the law, keeping the peace and upholding human rights. The question is, which human rights? This becomes a very arbitrary decision. The Macpherson report was actually very good. But when it got into the hands of the College of Policing it became less good, and since the College of Policing has been captured by ideologues, it has become next to useless.'

Role of the police

Miller's testimony points to the role of the police in applying, interpreting and agitating for hate speech legislation. The importance of police officers' decision-making, and identifying the perpetrators' motive, has been emphasised in relation to hate crime. We have also noted previously the role of the police in both determining and recording non-crime hate incidents. Operational guidance comes to police officers from the CoP, a professional body established in 2012. The CoP aims 'to provide those working in policing with the skills and knowledge necessary to prevent crime, protect the public, and secure public trust.' As a professional body it protects its members interests, for example representing Humberside Police in the High Court case against Miller detailed above.

The CoP responded directly to the statement made by Mr Justice Knowles in the case of *Miller v Humberside*, welcoming acknowledgement that:

> 'the mere recording of a non-crime hate incident based on an individual's speech is not an interference of their rights and if it was, it is prescribed by law and done for two of the legitimate aims in Article 10 of the European Convention on Human Rights (freedom of expression) and common law.'[65]

Deputy Chief Constable Bernie O'Reilly, said:

> 'The findings of the Stephen Lawrence Inquiry, on which some of our guidance was based, demonstrate the importance for us to understand how hate can escalate among communities. Our guidance is about protecting people because of who they are and we know this is an area where people may be reluctant to report things to us because of the very personal nature of what they experience or perceive.'[66]

Following *Miller v Humberside*, the CoP issued updated Hate Crime Operational Guidance so as to provide an explicit rationale for policing hate: 'These crime and non-crime incidents may have a disproportionate psychological, and in some cases physical, impact on victims and the wider community as compared to equivalent "non-hate" crimes.'

Involvement in 'non-crimes' that have a psychological impact on a wider community fundamentally redefines and substantially broadens the role of the police. Law enforcement becomes one task among many and is considered equivalent to a more explicitly political role of intervening to safeguard individuals and communities from offence.

The CoP guidance goes on to explain:

> 'Police officers and staff should respond positively to allegations, signs and perceptions of hostility and hate crime. Victims should be supported to make their allegation, they should be directed to sources of ongoing support and the matter should be recorded and flagged as a hate crime or non-crime hate incident.'

The use of the word 'victim' before allegations have been recorded, and a perpetrator found guilty suggests that simply the perception of having experienced hostility indicates you have been wronged. This is spelled out in the guidance which provides an expansive definition of hostility: 'In the absence of a precise legal definition of hostility, consideration should be given to ordinary dictionary definitions, which include ill-will, ill-feeling, spite, contempt, prejudice, unfriendliness, antagonism, resentment, and dislike.' There is also a prompt that:

> 'The victim does not have to justify or provide evidence of their belief, and police officers or staff should not directly challenge this perception. Evidence of the hostility is not required for an incident to be recorded as a hate crime or non-crime hate incident. A crime should be recorded as a hate crime or non-crime hate incident if it is perceived by the victim or any other person to be motivated by hostility.'

In addition: 'Any other person could refer to any one of a number of people, including: police officers or staff.'[67]

The capacity for police officers to perceive hate again changes the force's role from intervening in criminal (or potentially criminal) activity to participating in events so as to transform incidents into recordable offences. This paves the way for police officers who are led by subjective feelings rather than objective facts and enables the promotion of identity-based interests or favoured political causes. Indeed, the promotion of identity-based interests is organised through membership groups.

National Black Police Association

The National Black Police Association (NBPA) was formally established in 1998. However, its roots date back to 1990 and a joint initiative between black staff within the Metropolitan Police and a specialist support unit specialising in community and race relations training based in Bedfordshire led to the formation of a black support network. One particular concern was the high attrition rate of black officers. The NBPA goes substantially further and not only aims 'to improve the working environment of Black staff by protecting the rights of those employed within the Police Service', but also 'to enhance racial harmony and the quality of service to the Black community of the United Kingdom.'[68] This latter commitment arguably moves NBPA members away from a universal, colour-blind approach to policing.

Summer 2020 witnessed global protests in response to the killing in the US of a black man, George Floyd, at the hands of a police officer. From the UK, the NBPA issued a statement:

'From London, Birmingham and across the UK, the George Floyd incident is swelling simmering tensions. At a time when we are grappling with the harsh reality that decades of structural and institutional racism has made us fodder not only to the disproportionate use of force in policing but also to COVID19. Surely, now is the time for us to scramble to rid the world of the scourge of racism, structural and institutional with the same intensity as shown to COVID19. If we do not, what happened to George Floyd and the others before him, will yet again be shunted to the annals of race and policing history and what happened to George Floyd and the reaction to it, will be repeated across the world. The time has come to accept that racism is clearly the public health crisis, sadly shared by the USA and the UK. It is imperative that both nations need to act now.'[69]

This statement presents the existence of structural and institutional racism as an indisputable fact and claims the role of NBPA members is to 'rid the world' of this scourge in order to prevent a repeat of both the death of George Floyd and the reaction to it. This redefines the purpose of policing.

National LGBT+ Police Network[70]

The National LGBT+ Police Network plays a similar role to the NBPA in both protecting its members interests and advocating for broader social and political change. It is explicit about having a 'visible commitment' to members of the LGBTQ+ community both 'internally and externally.' The network urges members to demonstrate, 'to current trans staff and potential trans staff that you'll support them and value their contribution to your work. For example, include a clear statement of inclusivity and details of your trans policies on your website, communicate inclusive messages across social media channels and on your intranet.'[71] Again, we see that this dual role moves the network away from a straightforward defence of members' interests and into a more explicitly social and political public role. The National LGBT+ Police Network acknowledges the role of Stonewall in compiling its guidance: 'This guidance has been created by pulling together current guidance across the country, looking at real case studies and working closely with Stonewall.'[72]

As already noted, several police forces have registered as Stonewall Diversity Champions along with a wide range of other private sector and public institutions from the Post Office to Primark and from Adidas to the Army.[73] Stonewall has published a booklet: *Protecting Lesbian, Gay and Bisexual People, A practical guide for police forces*. It advises that 'Police forces need to take targeted action to tackle homophobic hate in their force area, encourage reporting and enable gay people to live without fear of abuse and violence.'[74] A major focus of the guide is how police officers can best ensure reporting of homophobic and transphobic hate crimes and hate incidents. Stonewall's reach into state funded organisations and reliance upon a perception of defending victims for securing revenue mean it has a vested interest in ensuring high levels of homophobic and transphobic hate crimes are recorded. Stonewall acts as a hate crime entrepreneur.

Law Professor Andrew Tettenborn explores the role of the police in relation to hate crime:

'It was around 2010 that the police really decided it was time they were seen to be doing something. The Association of Chief Police Officers (ACPO) decided they needed to be more involved in hate crime and that the best way to do this was to record as a hate incident anything perceived by the victim to be motivated by hate or contempt. But this definition of hate crime has no legal validity; it's purely the invention of a number of police forces. It's given support by ACPO, and the CPS also use it to show they mean business on hate crime, but there is no legal basis for it.'

'The police say they have no legal obligation to investigate only criminal offences. If someone is making a nuisance, the police can have a quiet word and tell them to stop, even if they are not breaking any laws. But they go further than this. If someone steps out of line, the police might tell them that the definition of a hate incident is anything perceived by the victim to be motivated by hate. There's no need to prove intent. So, they'll say if you don't stop, we will have to come to your house, arrest you, seize your computer and so on. This is how they deal with people who won't do as they are told.'

'When the government wants to be seen to be doing something more about more hate crime, it sends for the Law Commission. The Law Commission then carries out a survey and every activist contributes. Universities likewise advertise to recruit academics with an interest in hate crime. If you turn up for the interview and say this is a huge problem and we should get a grant from Stonewall to research it further, then you are far more likely to get a job than if you say there are no issues and you are worried about free speech. There is a distinct pecking order of human rights, and freedom of speech comes very low down it.'

Stonewall has influence not just with the police, but also in schools and with the CPS. It uses this influence to promote its own preferred definition of hate crime and to emphasise the importance of reporting hate crime. The Safe

Schools Alliance, a group of parents, teachers and health professionals concerned with safeguarding in schools, has expressed concern that the promotion of Stonewall's ideas around hate crime in schools may conflict with safeguarding objectives and place children at risk.

Safe Schools Alliance

'We first met online. We were all concerned about things that seemed to be happening in our children's schools and, in particular, the messages our children were getting about gender and sexuality. Much of it seemed to be linked to Stonewall and groups like Gendered Intelligence who promote the same message as Stonewall.'

'A group of about six of us decided to form the Safe Schools Alliance, with the aim of challenging equality and diversity policies in schools that didn't seem to be based on the law or to prioritise safeguarding. Our concern was that safeguarding was being overridden in a number of ways. For example, children were being told that they could use the toilets of the gender they identified with. We were also concerned that children were hearing it was acceptable to keep secrets from their parents. Schools were overriding protocols designed to keep children safe because they didn't fit with guidance from Stonewall. We don't think schools should bow down to ideology of any kind.'

'Freedom of speech is really important for safeguarding. This message has been made clear from a lot of case reviews, like the Warner Report. When people have raised concerns and they have been wrongly accused of being transphobic or racist, they have been

---

prevented from voicing legitimate worries. We cannot have a culture where people who are trying to protect children are shut down, because that is dangerous. We need an open, honest and transparent culture so we can focus on what's best for the child no matter what the prevailing ideology of the time.'

'Suddenly, we have a culture where safeguarding is equated with being hateful. Saying that a boy who identifies as a girl cannot use the girls' bathroom because of safeguarding issues is seen as being hateful to the whole transgender community because it implies that boys only become transgender in order to attack girls. This shuts down criticism. It tells you "you can't say that".'

'We welcomed Liz Truss' announcement about not changing the gender recognition act, but the battle is far from over. We are still concerned about affirmation, safeguarding, mental health and wellbeing. We still have a long way to go in schools. We want to challenge the fact that groups like Stonewall and Mermaids have so much influence in schools, for example, over PSHE resources. The Department of Education and the Equalities Office have all funded Stonewall and Mermaids without looking at what they are actually doing. It's like they've ticked a box in funding these organisations and that's it. No school should be a Stonewall champion. We are prioritising one very small group of people over others and it's actually to their detriment. There is still so much work to do.'

'We backed a teenage girl from Oxford who sought a judicial review of Oxfordshire County Council for recommending use of "the trans toolkit" in schools.

This guidance advised that children should be allowed to use the changing rooms and toilets of their preferred gender. The schoolgirl argued this guidance was unfair and made her feel powerless. A pre-action protocol was sent to Oxfordshire County Council, but they refused to withdraw the toolkit. That was when the claimant sought a judicial review, which was granted. However, Oxfordshire County Council pulled the toolkit instead of going to court.'

'The Crown Prosecution Service has itself compiled guidance for schools around hate crime in conjunction with Stonewall. This guidance has had a chilling effect on free speech and it sends girls the wrong message about personal boundaries. They are shown a picture of a transwoman who is very obviously male and asked about how she would feel if questioned about being in the wrong toilets. If people are worried about being accused of hate crimes then they don't feel able to raise legitimate concerns. So, this is one step on from social embarrassment at the prospect of being called out. You now risk having hate crime legislation thrown at you. The document says quite explicitly that people could be reported for hate crime if they question someone's right to be in a particular bathroom or changing room. 14-year-olds are threatened with being convicted of a hate crime.'

'Children are also taught that if you are a lesbian and you reject an advance from a transgender girl then you could be committing a hate crime. The complaint needn't come from the trans girl, it would be enough for someone else to think that you don't want to go out with that person because they are trans. You could still be accused of a hate crime. This is, quite literally, policing children's friendships. People think we are being alarmist when we point these things out, but they were all there in the CPS guidance to schools – and it was all backed by Stonewall.'

'Stonewall are essentially helping to shape CPS policy. This is a lobby group shaping policy which could end up becoming law. Another teenage girl sent a pre-action protocol to the CPS to get them to remove the hate speech guidance that had been written in conjunction with Stonewall. The CPS took their hate crime schools' guidance down while it was being reviewed. However, the claimant then pointed out that she didn't trust the CPS to review its own guidance as they were aligned with Stonewall through the Stonewall Champions Programme. So, she is now seeking a judicial review on the basis that the CPS should not be part of the Stonewall Champions Programme. We are now waiting to see if the judicial review will be granted.'

'This is huge. We have a teenage girl judicial reviewing the CPS and saying their policies are discriminatory and put her in danger. If this wins then it means that no other public body can align with Stonewall. The media are nervous about covering this – it's two very powerful organisations.'

'The police should not be partnering with any groups; their only role should be to uphold the law. What if the police decided to sign up to Extinction Rebellion or a pro-life group? It doesn't matter whether or not you agree with these groups – the police just shouldn't be taking sides. They should not be wearing rainbow lanyards, nothing.'

Hate Crime and Public Order (Scotland) Bill

The Hate Crime and Public Order (Scotland) Bill is currently making its way through the Scottish Parliament. This proposed legislation represents a first attempt within the UK to simplify the many disparate strands of law that criminalise hate or outlaw offence, compiled over decades. It aims to bring them together into one single piece of legislation that offers additional protection from hatred based on their age, sexual orientation, race, religion, disability or transgender identity. The bill emerges from the *Independent review of hate crime legislation in Scotland* – which was overseen by Lord Bracadale. Bracadale specifically calls for the addition of age and gender to the current list of protected characteristics.[75] In so doing, the bill, as it currently stands, extends current laws and criminalises a wider range of behaviour. It creates new offences relating to 'stirring up hatred' in relation to age, disability, religion, sexual orientation, transgender identity and race.

The Hate Crime and Public Order (Scotland) Bill has been criticised for the restrictions it will place on free speech. Writing in *The Spectator*, Stephen Daisley argues the proposed new law will criminalise anyone producing depictions of the Muslim prophet Mohammed (such as the French magazine Charlie Hebdo). Daisley points to the impact of a new offence of 'stirring up hatred', which is committed when anyone 'behaves in a threatening or abusive manner, or communicates threatening or abusive material to another person' on the basis of 'religion or, in the case of a social or cultural group, perceived religious affiliation'. The likelihood of being prosecuted under this proposed new legislation is compounded by the fact that no evidence is needed of intent or actual hatred being 'stirred up': 'Merely behaving or communicating in a way deemed "likely" to stir up hatred will be enough.' In addition, 'possessing inflammatory material', defined as 'threatening or abusive material with a view to communicating the material to another person' will also be criminalised.[76]

The historian and archaeologist Neil Oliver, writing in *The Sunday Times*, argues that the Hate Crime Bill not only poses 'a sinister threat to free speech', but also a threat to 'everything it means to be Scottish.' He points to widespread opposition to the bill from within Scotland. The Law Society and the Faculty of Advocates have warned that the proposed offence of 'stirring up hatred' based on 'religion or, in the case of social or cultural group, perceived religious affiliation' is 'vague and likely to create difficulty'. The Law Society has expressed concern that 'even an actor's performance, which might well be deemed insulting or offensive, could result in a criminal conviction under the terms of the bill'.[77]

Rather than clarifying what is and is not against the law, the proposed bill risks introducing a new vagueness into legislation. The Scottish Police Federation, which represents 98 per cent of officers, has said the legislation would leave officers no option but to 'police what people think or feel,' a move that it says would 'devastate the legitimacy of the police in the eyes of the public'. The federation said it could cause 'a significant increase in police workload and demand', complicating the law with new rules which are 'too vague to be implemented'.[78] In addition, 20 comedians, artists and authors, including the crime writer Val McDermid and comedian Rowan Atkinson, signed a letter warning that the new laws could have a 'stifling' effect on freedom of speech.[79] Even the Scottish wing of the Labour Party has criticised the bill.

In a Submission in Opposition to the Proposed Bill, Carlton Brick, a lecturer in Sociology at the University of the West of

Scotland, argues that as well as having dire consequences for free speech, the increasingly punitive nature of the Bill will have adverse impacts upon the Scottish criminal justice system:

'Scotland appears to be becoming Europe's carceral capital, the Hate Crime Bill will make this appearance a reality. This regressive tendency is likely to be exacerbated by two principle elements of the proposed bill: the increase in sentencing for "proven" hate crimes; and the lowering of the threshold of "proof" (for example section 1(1)(b) which "does not require there to be a specific victim"; and section 1(4) that "provides that collaboration is not required to prove that an offence was aggravated by prejudice".'

Brick notes that, most fundamentally, 'the proposed Bill undermines the equality implicit in law required to protect a diverse society.' He argues:

'Equality is not the same as fairness – indeed equality may often seem "unfair" i.e. that it treats subjects as equal (the same) despite "obvious differences" and "different abilities" – in particular spheres these differences are "equalised" through measures that seek to "level out" the inequality (for example work legislation). However, in the spheres of democracy and law the unconditional and non-discriminatory nature of equality is most important. Democracies are dependent upon the idea that regardless of class, economic or educational status for example each member's opinion and vote carries equal weight. Likewise, central to the equality of law is the notion that it does not discriminate – it is "blind" to status. However, once the law begins to discriminate and treat sections of society differently, it institutionalises inequality and moves from a society of free individuals bound by the rule of law, towards a society of unfree individuals bound by law and nothing else.'

Oliver points out that the proposed new law is the 'passion project' of Humza Yousaf, the Scottish National Party's (SNP) 35-year-old justice secretary. Yousaf claimed, in response to criticism, that the Scottish government was 'absolutely explicit' that freedom of expression was not under attack, and was committed to 'ensuring Scotland is a place where there is zero tolerance of hate crime'.[80] Nonetheless, on September 23rd the Scottish government announced that the Hate Crime Bill would be amended to ease concerns over its impact on free speech. The original legislation could have seen people prosecuted under new 'stirring up hatred' offences, if stirring up hatred was considered to be a 'likely consequence', despite never having been the intention of the speaker. The bill will now be amended so it only applies to people who *intend* to stir up hate.[81]

Brick points to broader changes within Scottish politics as having motivated the Hate Crime and Public Order (Scotland) Bill. 'An elite within the Scottish National Party (SNP) are increasingly moving away from pushing for independence and repositioning themselves according to a far more woke and identitarian agenda.' This, Brick explains, creates a split within the independence movement: 'Sturgeon is a problem because she is not pushing for independence as much as some older members of the party would like. Instead, she is situating the SNP within identitarian movements and this is the focus of the Hate Crime Bill.'[82]

The roots of this divide, Brick explains, extend over decades.

'From the 1980s there were moves to professionalise and modernise the SNP. In practice, this meant distancing the party's leadership from the members. This came to a head with Salmond's leadership. The SNP were shocked to lose the independence referendum, but post-2014 party membership actually increased. It's now the second biggest party in Europe but the members now are different to the type of people the party used to attract. They are generally younger and surveys show they are far more concerned with social justice and particular issues like trans rights. Sturgeon, as leader, brought with her a plan to move away from the old politics and follow the interests of these new members.'

Brick points out that one problem for the 'new' SNP is that it 'has not got organic roots in society, it's got no constituency.' Andrew Tettenborn concurs: 'Sturgeon's constituency is people in the wealthy suburbs of Glasgow and Edinburgh. He'll be a surgeon, she'll be a deputy headteacher. They'll be the best paid people around. And these are the people the SNP want to keep onside. The rest of the population fall into line because there's no real opposition to the SNP.'

Instead, Brick suggests, the SNP uses proposed legislation as a means of identifying potential allies:

'The identity based bodies quoted in the document are funded by the Scottish government – so the process becomes cyclical. The advising bodies tell the government what it wants to hear. They also pull on sections of academia, particularly in Edinburgh. They are looking to academia for a constituency but it's fragile, it has no real roots in society.'

He adds:

'What comes across most strongly as driving this demand for new legislation is just the SNP's complete contempt for ordinary people, for what they perceive to be Scottish society. This is why they are not a credible nationalist party because their whole premise is that Scottish society is terrible.'

The SNP turn to hate crime entrepreneurs, rather than citizens, as a source of legitimacy.

The absence of a broader constituency for the SNP's ideas

offers one explanation for the criticism the Hate Crime Bill (Scotland) has faced from such a vast array of people and institutions. Brick, however, sounds a note of caution:

'Opposition to the Hate Crime Bill is entirely focused around the issue of free speech. There is no opposition to the identitarian move to take us away from equality before the law. Once social differences are reflected in legal precedents then people no longer have recourse to equality before the law. This is the issue at stake here and it is what a previous generation of activists fought for. Yet the briefing documents that go with the Bill don't mention equality at all, they talk about diversity. Diversity is the key phrase. Equality, as a term, has been so disfigured from its Enlightenment meaning that, as a concept, it's been rendered meaningless.'[83]

Professor Andrew Tettenborn concurs:

'If you give one protected group the right to suppress speech they don't like then you have to give it to all of them, regardless of whether or not they experience any problems. This is the thinking behind the Scottish proposals. Lord Bracadale's report employs this exact logic. But the upshot is we no longer have equality before the law. This means that two victims will be treated differently even if they both have the exact same injuries. Crime should be crime irrespective of the motive.'[84]

2.

Law Commission Consultation Paper 250: Hate Crime Laws

As we have seen, there is no one piece of legislation that details hate crime and the criminalisation of hate speech. Instead, the law emerges from multiple Acts of Parliament passed over a period of several decades. As a result, the Law Commission notes that 'England and Wales has one of the most comprehensive hate crime reporting and recording systems in the world.' Despite this, it is widely recognised that this complexity creates gaps and inconsistencies in the law, as well as making it 'unnecessarily difficult to communicate to the public generally, and harder for police to implement in practice.'[85] In response, both the Scottish Parliament and the UK government are now looking to 'tidy up' hate crime and hate speech laws through bringing together disparate acts into one coherent piece of legislation. As previously noted, the Hate Crime and Public Order Bill is currently making its way through the Scottish Parliament, while the UK government has asked the Law Commission to consult on changes to the law in England and Wales.

The remit for the Law Commission's consultation is set out as follows:

'We are consulting on hate crime and hate speech laws in in England and Wales: in particular the aggravated offences regime under sections 28 to 32 of the Crime and Disorder

Act 1998, the enhanced sentencing regime under sections 145 and 146 of the Criminal Justice Act 2003, the "stirring up" offences under Parts 3 and 3A of the Public Order Act 1986, and the offence of "racialist chanting" contrary to section 3(1) of the Football Offences Act 1991. The consultation will focus on two main questions: 1. Who should these laws protect? 2. How should these laws work?'

The consultation notes that a 'flurry of legislative activity has resulted in a significant volume of hate crime laws,' but that this has created a situation where laws are 'overly complex and draw arbitrary distinctions between the different communities they protect.' It points to an additional problem of definition:

'Hatred is not defined in the Public Order Act 1986, and can be taken to bear its ordinary meaning. [...] As a term which appears very rarely in criminal statutes, there is limited further definition in case law, and it is ultimately a question for the jury whether this standard has been met.'

The consultation notes that the definition of hate used by the police and the CPS for monitoring purposes is 'significantly wider ... than the legal tests that apply to offences and sentencing under the relevant hate crime legislation, which require proof that the offence was motivated by or the offender demonstrated hostility based on the characteristic (or presumed characteristic).'[86]

The consultation outlines four key arguments that have been associated with punishing hate crimes more severely than differently motivated crimes:

1. Hate crime causes additional harm, namely to primary victims, but also to groups who share the targeted characteristic and to society more widely. It leaves communities feeling vulnerable to further victimisation.

2. Hate crime constitutes greater intrinsic wrongdoing.

3. Hate crime offenders are more culpable than those who commit equivalent offences which are not hate crimes.

4. More severe punishment sends out a message, denouncing the hatred as wrong.

These arguments reflect the theoretical assumptions of the many academics cited in the report.

The Law Commission points to a number of 'key concerns' and criticisms with the current approach to hate crime laws:

1. The disparity in the way that the existing five characteristics are protected in law. Groups who are protected to a lesser degree – notably LGBT and disabled people – argue that this is wrong in principle, and has a damaging effect in practice.

2. The lack of clarity in the current laws, which are spread across several different statutes, and do not operate consistently across the characteristics which are protected.

3. The particularly low level of prosecution of disability hate crime, relative both to the number of disabled people in the community, and the extent to which they are targeted for criminal conduct.

4. Arguments that the law should expand to include new categories to counter various other forms of hatred and prejudice in society – notably misogyny and ageism – and hostility towards other targeted groups such as homeless people, sex workers and alternative subcultures. The language used for some of the existing categories – notably the current legal definition of 'transgender' – was also criticised.

5. Concerns around the enforcement of hate crime laws, with inconsistent practices amongst police, prosecutors and the judiciary the cause of some concern.

6. Barriers to reporting faced by certain groups. These can include the sheer scale and normalisation of the abuse, a lack of trust in law enforcement agencies, and specific fears – such as the fear of 'outing' faced by some members of the LGBT community.

7. The limitations of a purely criminal justice response, and the need to tackle the causes of hate crime and provide adequate support for victims.

In seeking to tackle these concerns, the Law Commission notes: 'A strong case has been made to us for change to the law, so that the current "motivation" limb does not require evidence at the high threshold of "hostility"', acknowledging that this 'would represent a significant shift in the way hate crime is conceived of and dealt with in England and Wales. It could potentially result in the prosecution of hate crimes in circumstances where the perpetrator neither holds nor demonstrates any particular animosity towards the characteristic.'[87]

In addition, the authors of the consultation propose that the criteria to determine whether a characteristic is included in hate crime laws should be:

1. Demonstrable need: evidence that crime based on hostility or prejudice towards the group is prevalent.

2. Additional Harm: there is evidence that criminal targeting based on hostility or prejudice towards the characteristic causes additional harm to the victim, members of the targeted group, and society more widely.

3. Suitability: protection of the characteristic would fit logically within the broader offences and sentencing framework, prove workable in practice, represent an efficient use of criminal justice resources, and is consistent with the rights of others.

The combined effect of lowering the threshold of 'hostility' and broadening the criteria for protected characteristics will be to bring far more people into contact with the police and criminalise a far wider range of speech and behaviour.

Race

We have already noted that the earliest hate crime legislation, enacted in the UK in 1965, was designed to prohibit 'incitement to racial hatred'. In practice, this meant that racially aggravated crime could be punished more severely than crime not shown to have a racist motivation, and racist speech considered likely to incite violence was made unlawful. In the decades after this legislation was passed, there was a growing sense that it set the bar too high for criminalisation and did not allow police to record incidents of racist speech that were neither attached to criminal activity nor could be deemed 'incitement'. The Macpherson report into the murder of Stephen Lawrence recommended adopting a far broader definition of 'racist incidents' and called for better recording and reporting of racist crimes. As the Law Commission's Consultation Paper notes: 'This led to a number of local and national initiatives aimed at improving the criminal justice system's operational response to hate crime.'[88] In addition, the Macpherson report prompted a discussion about institutional racism within the police service and other public bodies.

In recent years, new definitions of racism have come to the fore. 'Systemic' racism has largely replaced the concept of 'institutional' racism. The idea of systemic racism emerges from critical race theory and suggests that racism is so embedded within culture that it colonises the unconscious minds of white people. Furthermore, according to critical race theory, the harm of racist speech goes far beyond 'incitement' to hatred or violence. Instead, racist speech is itself an act of harm, and even violence.

In discussing racist hate speech, the Law Commission's Consultation draws heavily upon key proponents of critical race theory. The authors cite academics and researchers who point to the 'background of oppression' and 'historical disadvantage' suffered by black people in the UK to argue that the 'wound' caused by hate speech is experienced more severely in this context. In addition, it is argued that 'race-based hostility is more harmful, as it targets a more fundamental component of the person's identity, and compounds the impact of other manifestations of discrimination and disadvantage that affect racial minorities.'

Other research cited reinforces the idea that the centrality of race to a person's identity compounds the harm of racist speech: 'hate crime's distinct harm stems from the victim's perception of their experience as an attack upon the core of their identity.' The 'values of the attacker' are assumed to be inherent in hate speech, and it is 'the values of the attacker striking at the core of the victim's identity' that cause harm. Elsewhere it is claimed that 'hate crimes can cause more harm because they invoke past and ongoing discrimination.' This assumes that:

> 'crime serves as a painful reminder of the cultural heritage of past and ongoing discrimination, stereotyping and stigmatization of their identity group. When an anti-black racist hate crime occurs it brings all of the dormant feelings of

anger, fear and pain to the collective psychological forefront of the victim. This is not the case when whites are the target of racist hate crime.'

Critical race theory makes clear that black and white people do not experience words attacking them on the basis of their racial identity in the same way. The context of 'past and ongoing discrimination' means that the same attacking words will be experienced differently by white and black people, and be more harmful to black people. The consultation suggests it is necessary:

'to consider alternative ways for such groups to evidence additional harm. These might include the subordination of identity characteristics and compounding the effects of pre-existing disadvantage. Both of these factors are causally linked to additional harm and might be used by victims to articulate the significant level of harm that they experience as a result of crime that is linked to prejudice or hostility towards their characteristic.'

Arguing that the same words cause different levels of harm in black and white people, the Law Commission are rejecting equality before the law. They are asking for people to be treated differently, according to the colour of their skin, despite experiencing the same objective circumstances. The assumption that black people will experience greater harm because of historical oppression suggests black people are more sensitive and have a deeper-rooted connection to the past than white people. It also risks suggesting that black people are less resilient and less in control of their emotional responses than white people, and that this greater degree of emotionality needs to be acknowledged in the law.

The Law Commission's proposed changes will lower the bar for hate speech. Any comment that is perceived to be an attack on a person's racial identity, regardless of the actual words used or the intention of the speaker, will be assumed to be hate speech. Introducing greater subjectivity into the law, combined with a differential response based upon the skin colour of the victim/perpetrator, risks enshrining racial inequality in law. This could lead to greater criminalisation of white people and, at the same time, an understanding of black people as psychologically more vulnerable to provocation.

Misogyny

The Law Commission's Consultation on Hate Crime Law proposes that gender or sex should be a protected characteristic for the purposes of hate crime law, although much of the preamble to this proposal centres around the issue of misogyny. This reflects the fact that the Hate Crime (Misogyny) Bill is currently going through Parliament. This bill, introduced by Wera Hobhouse MP, seeks to make 'motivation by misogyny an aggravating factor in criminal sentencing and to require police forces to record hate crimes motivated by misogyny'. It has the widespread backing of a number of feminist campaign groups and prominent individuals such as the Fawcett Society, Citizens UK and Stella Creasy MP. The proposed bill, and the Law Commission Consultation, focus on misogyny rather than sex on the assumption that women form the majority of sex or gender-based hate crime victims.

A similar bill that seeks to criminalise misandry as well as misogyny is also due a second parliamentary reading before the end of this year.[89] Meanwhile, the Hate Crime and Public Order (Scotland) Bill lays the foundations for criminalising those who stir up hatred on the basis of sex through the inclusion of a power allowing its introduction by extra-parliamentary ministerial order at a later stage.[90]

Arguments for misogyny to be made a hate crime are backed by statistics reporting to show high levels of abuse directed at women and, perhaps more controversially, a link between verbal harassment or misogynistic attitudes more generally, and other criminal activity. The abuse women are described as experiencing ranges from 'verbal and nonverbal street remarks to incidents of stalking and physical assaults.' Nottinghamshire Police Force began recording misogynistic hate crimes in 2016. According to the Law Commission, between April 2016 and March 2018, 174 women reported crimes ranging from verbal abuse to sexual assault, of which 73 were classified as hate crimes and 101 were classified as hate incidents.

Violent and sexual acts committed against women are already, rightly, criminal offences. Murder, rape, sexual assault, stalking, domestic abuse and coercive control all fall under the jurisdiction of existing laws. In addition, 'verbal and nonverbal street remarks' may, as the Law Commission acknowledge,

> 'amount to either the offence of "harassment, alarm or distress" under section 5 of the Public Order Act 1986, or the more serious offence of "intentional harassment, alarm or distress" under section 4A of the same Act. If it occurs on more than one occasion, harassment or stalking offences under the Protection of Harassment Act 1997 may also apply.'[91]

Despite existing laws, campaigning organisations point to new forms or sites of harassment of women. The Law Commission highlights a 2018 report from the Equality and Human Rights Commission that notes the prevalence of sexual harassment in UK workplaces, citing research claiming that 40 per cent of women have experienced some form of unwanted sexual behaviour in the workplace.

One problem with such research is that 'sexual behaviour' is often defined so broadly as to encompass everything from sexual assault to overhearing an inappropriate joke. As a result, the Women and Equalities Committee of the House of Commons concluded in 2018 that 'sexual harassment affects the lives of nearly every woman in the UK.'

Women are also considered more likely than men to be the target of online harassment and abuse. The Law Commission cite Amnesty International's 'Toxic Twitter' research which argued that:

> 'in the case of online violence and abuse, women of colour, religious or ethnic minority women, lesbian, bisexual, transgender or intersex (LBTI) women, women with disabilities, or non-binary individuals who do not conform to traditional gender norms of male and female, will often experience abuse that targets them in unique or compounded way.'[92]

The treatment of female MPs is a particular concern of the Law Commission. Its consultation points out that, 'In the six weeks before the 2017 UK general election, 45% of all abusive tweets sent to female MPs were directed at Diane Abbott MP – the UK's first black female MP' and 'In 2018, Jess Phillips MP said she received 600 online "rape threats" in one evening. This followed comments made by Carl Benjamin, who stood as a Member of the European Parliament (MEP) candidate for the UK Independence Party (UKIP), that he "wouldn't even bother" to rape Jess Phillips.'[93]

The conclusion that almost all women are victims of sexual harassment in almost every sphere of their lives is evidenced through broad-based, subjective, advocacy research of the kind undertaken by Amnesty International into women's experiences of social media. Yet despite the contested nature of the conclusions reached, it is assumed that commonplace 'prejudicial ideas' about ideas about women are 'closely connected' to violence against women and girls. Much of the same thinking behind expanding race-based hate crime underpins the proposal to make misogyny a hate crime. The Law Commission points to the Istanbul Convention which recognises: 'that violence against women is a manifestation of historically unequal power relations between men and women, which have led to domination over and discrimination against women by men and to the prevention of the full advancement of women.' The areas in which women have yet to achieve 'full advancement' are not specified.

All women are presented as sharing a common experience of womanhood, which means that even though differences are acknowledged, 'depending on race, gender identity, religion, sexual orientation, disability status and class,' at a broader level, 'women are collectively affected by the prevalence and normalised nature of VAWG [violence against women and girls] in society, even if they themselves are not primary victims.' In other words, if one woman is attacked, then all women are assumed to feel more vulnerable as a result. This is spelled out:

> 'Gender-bias crimes affect women collectively, similar to the way that burning a cross or vandalizing a synagogue affects an entire racial or religious community. The act does not just affect one individual; rather, it affects an entire group, making the targeted community feel fear and, sometimes, a sense of inferiority.'[94]

The assumption that all women experience sexual harassment and that this harassment is a manifestation of historically unequal power relations means that, despite existing legislation criminalising sexual discrimination, sexual harassment and all forms of violence against women and girls, the Law Commission argues that the law must be extended still further. The Consultation paper argues against broader sex-based protections, noting:

> 'the wealth of research and scholarship that connects sexual offences and domestic abuse perpetrated by men against women on a micro level, to the fact that social norms and practices accept and sustain male domination and female subordination at a macro level. There is no equivalent dynamic that subordinates the broad category of "men" and sustains the domination of the broad category of "women" at a macro level.'

There are reasons to be concerned about both the proposal to make gender or sex a protected characteristic for the purposes of hate crime law and the proposal to criminalise misogyny. One risk is that, with broad and subjective definitions of harassment, almost every interaction between men and women could be subject to policing. The Law Commission's proposals seem premised on a belief that women are an oppressed minority in society today. This takes no account of the legal equality and tremendous social progress women have made. While it is the case that some women are no doubt disadvantaged today, the experiences of different women vary enormously. Sex-based legal protections cannot take account of these differences. Existing laws already, rightly, prohibit sexual violence and harassment. Proposals to expand the law seem driven by a desire to 'send a message' about the importance of protecting women. The risk is that using the law in this way criminalises men and tells women they are victims in a hostile society.

The Law Commission's proposals would do nothing to protect women in one area where misogynistic abuse is rampant today: in discussion around the biological reality of being female and women's sex-based rights. As we have seen in the interview with Caroline Farrow (above), women who challenge the idea that 'trans women are women' and defend female-only spaces and provisions can face not just verbal abuse, but physical violence.[95] Yet the Law Commission's proposals not only do nothing to protect women in such instances but, worse, would further brand them as perpetrators of hate crime against people on the basis of their gender identity. In discussing which philosophical beliefs should be protected under the law, the Commission emphasise 'the requirement that a protected belief be "worthy of respect in a democratic society and not incompatible with human dignity or in conflict with the fundamental rights of others",' noting that 'this necessarily excludes 'objectionable' political philosophies.' 'Objectionable political philosophies' are said to include 'racist or homophobic' beliefs, as well as '"absolutist" views of sex.' Understanding women and girls to be female, and distinct from men and boys who are male, would be described as fact by many scientists and members of the public, and not an 'absolutist' viewpoint.

Transgender

The Law Commission's Consultation Paper proposes extending existing hate crime legislation to offer greater protection to transgender people. The authors express concern with the definition of transgender referred to in existing legislation. They argue 'the current definition places significant emphasis on the process of gender reassignment, rather than on the identity and personhood of the individual.'

The consultation paper draws instead upon a definition of transgender provided by the advocacy group Stonewall: 'An umbrella term to describe people whose gender is not the same as, or does not sit comfortably with, the sex they were assigned at birth.' This definition, despite being presented neutrally in an introductory glossary, is highly contested. Most biologists, scientists and doctors would disagree that sex is 'assigned at birth,' in some seemingly random process, but would suggest instead that sex is formed *in utero* and is inscribed in a fetus' chromosomes long before birth.

Drawing upon work by Stonewall and other charities and campaigning groups that represent transgender people, the Law Commission proposes revising the current definition of transgender in hate crime laws to include:

- People who are or are presumed to be transgender;

- People who are or are presumed to be non-binary;

- People who cross dress (or are presumed to cross dress);

- People who are or are presumed to be intersex.

The authors recognise that a definition this broad extends far beyond people who have or about to undergo gender reassignment. They propose instead a new category: 'transgender, non-binary or intersex'. Nonetheless, the consultation paper makes clear that even this broad grouping may eventually fall foul of linguistic updates:

> 'We recognise that as understandings of gender identity and sex characteristics evolve, so does terminology. We therefore welcome input from consultees on language which is inclusive, appropriate, and likely to remain so into the future.'[96]

Clearly, defining transgender as a matter of 'identity' rather than 'gender reassignment' draws considerably greater numbers of people under the protection of the law. Indeed, it is on the basis of crimes committed against this larger group that expansion of the law is justified. The concept of 'relative prevalence' considers the likelihood of a member of a particular group becoming the victim of a hate crime by dividing the number of crimes committed against the total group membership. In this way, transgender people are considered to be more in need of protection than older people. In the year 2018/19, the CPS recorded 2958 prosecutions for crimes committed against older people out of an estimated population size of almost 12 million people aged 65 or over.

> 'By contrast, in 2018/19 there were 2,333 police recorded hate crime and incidents against transgender people, who make up a much smaller group (whilst no robust data on the UK trans population exists, in 2018 the Government tentatively estimated that there were approximately 200,000-500,000 trans people in the UK).'[97]

According to this calculation, transgender people are far more at risk than older people. However, it is worth noting that this comparison draws upon two different sets of statistics. The number of successful prosecutions of crimes committed against older people is compared to the far lower standard of 'recorded hate crimes and hate incidents' committed against transgender people.

The Law Commission further cites statistics gathered by Stonewall which claim that '41 per cent of trans people and 31 per cent of non-binary people have experienced a hate crime or incident because of their gender identity in the last 12 months.' As noted previously, Stonewall acts as a 'hate crime entrepreneur'. The more it can demonstrate that its members are victims of hate crime, the more public sympathy, influence and, ultimately, money it can generate. To this end, Stonewall actively solicits reports of hate crime with no expectation of corroborating evidence. Stonewall justifies this approach on the basis of, 'testimony we heard from trans individuals, several of whom stated that they report only a fraction of the abuse they receive to the police.'[98]

As with race and sex, calls to expand hate crime legislation are premised on the significance of group identity and the belief that an attack on an individual has a broader impact on all community members. Following a hate crime, we are told 'individuals or groups who share the targeted characteristic can feel wary of their surroundings and question their safety.' One academic cited by the Law Commission claims this group injury is 'particularly stark in transgender communities', quoting as evidence one trans woman who says, 'it only has to happen once or twice and that really affects, you know, and I think it has affected the overall community, right?'[99]

The focus on group membership within proposed legislation suggests law enforcement is as much concerned with recognition and affirmation of identity as it is about protecting or punishing individuals. This demand for recognition throws up new legal challenges. For example, if the activist mantra that 'trans women are women' is accepted, then the need for an additional category of hate crime to capture the experiences of trans women should not be necessary. The Law Commission clarify this point:

'To use a non-binary person as an example, where they are targeted because of hostility towards their non-binary gender, we think this is more appropriately characterised as hatred based on a person's transgender or non-binary identity, than misogynistic hatred. Conversely, where a non-binary person is perceived by an offender to be a woman and targeted based on hostility towards their (perceived) female gender, this could be characterised as misogynistic hatred.'[100]

In its consultation, the Law Commission uses a highly contested definition of transgender provided by Stonewall, an activist group representing the interests of transgender people. This, we can assume, is considered best practice for drawing upon the 'lived experiences' of the group in question. The uncritical use of testimony from hate crime entrepreneurs means that legal changes are being proposed not on the basis of objective evidence, but on the subjective demands of activists for recognition and affirmation of suffering. In this way, the law becomes politicised.

Equality before the law

Equality before the law is an important, longstanding and hard-won right. This principle demands all citizens be treated equally – irrespective of their sex, skin colour or sexuality. Of course, equality before the law does not take account of historic or present disadvantage or discrimination. Nor does it imply equality of outcome. It does mean that the law will not treat people differently on the basis of who they are.

Hate crime legislation ends equality before the law. Rather than treating people equally, irrespective of race, sex or sexuality, it does the exact opposite and insists that these characteristics of a person's identity are made central to any legal dispute by acting as the basis for determining whether a crime has or has not been committed. Comparable crimes are no longer treated similarly based on the objective facts surrounding the offence, but are instead treated differently depending upon the identity of the victim.

As previously noted, critics of current hate crime legislation are unlikely to argue for the principle of equality, but instead make the case for 'levelling up' protections to be extended to additional groups, such as homeless people and sex workers. The Law Commission's Consultation points to the fact that 'Differential treatment of the characteristics currently protected under hate crime laws has been a persistent criticism in our consultation meetings.' It shares concerns from disability groups and LGBT groups 'about unequal treatment in law compared with race and religion, and the practical and symbolic implications of this.' The Law Commission's response is to reiterate conclusions from their 2014 report in which they:

> 'found that "it is undesirable for the current law to give the impression of a 'hierarchy' of victims" and that unless there is some good reason to limit the protection of aggravated offences to race and religion "it is unacceptable for the same system not to apply to all five characteristics."'

This becomes an argument, not for equality before the law for all citizens, but instead for equality only among members of different victim groups. As the Law Commission makes clear:

> 'our provisional view is that there are enough common features among the existing protected characteristics such that the law should seek to provide equal protection to all of them. This would represent a departure from the current approach, which is inconsistent, and creates a "hierarchy of hate" amongst protected groups. We believe a consistent approach would make hate crime laws both clearer and fairer.'[101]

The Law Commission recognises the challenge hate crime legislation poses to equality before the law. It responds to criticism thus:

> 'While we understand the genuinely held concerns of those who subscribe to this view, we do not accept this conclusion.

The law recognises that the same base offence may be more or less serious in different circumstances. The only crime for which the penalty is fixed by law is murder, and even for murder judges are expected to take into account the particular circumstances when setting the minimum term to be served before the offender is eligible to apply for parole. Moreover, hate crime laws in England and Wales turn on the motivation for the offence, or the demonstration of hostility, not the identity of the victim: the law does not, for instance, treat a black victim differently from a white victim, or a gay offender differently from a heterosexual offender.'

There are a number of problems with this response. Taking into account the particular circumstances of a crime does not call equality before the law into question if the process is applied objectively to all crimes of the same type, irrespective of the identity of victim or perpetrator. While hate crime turns on the demonstration of hostility, it is disingenuous to say all victims are treated alike. It would be far harder for a white victim, for example, to prove race-based hostility than a black victim. In justifying extending hate crime law on account of the historical disadvantage experienced by different groups, the Law Commission potentially takes us further down this path.

Indeed, the Law Commission acknowledges that, in some instances:

'protection is afforded to only a subset of a wider category (in these cases the wider groups might be framed as "ability" and "gender identity") and there is a clear distinction with those who are not protected: ie non-disabled and cisgender people.'

They argue for a broader approach to offer greater protection to more people, for example, 'to remove the disparity between each of the protected characteristics, so that Muslims, Jews, Sikhs, Christians and other religious groups enjoy equivalent protection, regardless of whether they are classified as a racial group, religious group, or both.' However, the 'need for a broad approach' is clearly a practical, rather than principled position:

> 'The need for a broad approach is somewhat less apparent in respect of sexual orientation, where it might be possible to exclude "heterosexual" people from protection on the basis that there is little evidence that this group is targeted for hate crime. However, the increasing recognition of the complexity of human sexuality, and the emergence of new identities such as pansexuality would likely render a stark binary distinction somewhat difficult in practice.'

And not one that will be extended to all groups 'to extend the protected characteristic to "a disability (or presumed disability, or presumed lack of disability)". The intention would not be to provide protection to ablebodied persons, but rather to ensure the inclusion of disabled persons who are perceived by the perpetrator either not to be disabled, or not "disabled enough".'[102]

Instead, the Consultation recommends 'that the protection offered by aggravated offences should extend equally across all the protected hate crime characteristics' (that is, not additional characteristics) with the aim of achieving 'greater parity of protection, beginning with a consistent approach to the characteristics protected by aggravated offences.' Equality is redefined as an equality of victimhood (for some) when the law comes to relate to vast swathes of the population as citizens in need of protection.

This view of equality is in keeping with the theoretical underpinnings of the consultation and draws heavily upon critical legal theory (CLT). CLT has been defined as:

'a theory which states that the law is necessarily intertwined with social issues, particularly stating that the law has inherent social biases. Proponents of CLS believe that the law supports the interests of those who create the law. As such, CLS states that the law supports a power dynamic which favors the historically privileged and disadvantages the historically underprivileged.'[103]

Critical legal theorists argue that abandoning equality before the law, and treating people differently, is necessary to create equality in a social context in which some groups are more likely to suffer discrimination and disadvantage. The Law Commission make this point explicitly:

'hate crime can cause harm to wider society – for example by damaging the principle of equality. For the purposes of measuring this, we establish two ways that this damage might occur. Firstly, criminal targeting might decrease social cohesion – leading to the isolation or withdrawal of vulnerable communities, reinforcing outsider status for certain groups or deepening tensions and divisions between different groups. Secondly, this criminal targeting might undermine a group's equal participation in economic, social, political and cultural life.'[104]

In this way, legal inequality is thought necessary to promote social equality. However, this fundamentally alters the role of the law from neutral arbiter to an active and explicitly biased participant in disputes.

Free expression

Britain has no equivalent of the US first amendment to protect free speech. Instead, such protections that do exist stem from the European Commission on Human Rights (ECHR). Article 10 of the ECHR states:

'Everyone has the right to freedom of expression. This right shall include freedom to hold opinions and to receive and impart information and ideas without interference by public authority and regardless of frontiers [...] The exercise of these freedoms, since it carries with it duties and responsibilities, may be subject to such formalities, conditions, restrictions or penalties as are prescribed by law and are necessary in a democratic society, in the interests of national security, territorial integrity or public safety, for the prevention of disorder or crime, for the protection of health or morals, for the protection of the reputation or rights of others.'[105]

Although beginning with a clear indication of rights, much of this statement is taken up with qualifications and exceptions to free expression. The UK's hate crime and hate speech legislation comfortably qualifies as an exception under the need to ensure public safety, the prevention of disorder or crime, the protection of health or morals and the protection of the reputation or the rights of others.

As well as ending equality before the law, the Law Commission's proposed changes to hate crime legislation further curtail free expression. The Law Commission acknowledges the importance of free expression but then states:

'this is an area of law where a balance has to be struck between intervention and freedom of speech; that there are strong views on all sides of the argument; and that it will be an important task of the Law Commission, when considering responses to this consultation, to identify the principles which should guide that balance.'[106]

Unfortunately for the Commission, speech cannot be a 'little bit' free. If the law is to 'intervene' to ensure a 'balance', then we do not have free expression but state-approved expression. Unsurprisingly then, the Law Commission's proposals would limit what can and cannot be said far more severely than at present. As is made clear, their starting point is that 'hate speech laws can represent a permissible interference with freedom of expression.'

As previously noted, the Law Commission presents an understanding of speech, and expression more broadly, which is in keeping with the tenets of CLT. According to CLT, speech should be restricted because words can be intrinsically harmful and wound individuals in ways comparable to an act of physical violence. In addition, words can harm the collective dignity of a targeted group and prevent its members from fully participating in society.

Those who campaign for free expression are particularly concerned with offences of 'stirring up' hatred. There are currently two sets of 'stirring up' offences:

- Those relating to stirring up racial hatred, which involve: (a) threatening, abusive or insulting words or material (b) intended or likely to stir up racial hatred;

- Those relating to religious hatred or hatred on grounds of sexual orientation, which involve: (a) threatening words or material (b) intended to stir up hatred.[107]

In both instances, 'stirring up' is defined broadly and encompasses words and behaviour in images and written material, recordings, broadcasts and theatrical productions. This includes general statements, not directed at individuals, but commenting on groups of people. Significantly, prosecution for 'stirring up' does not require 'proof that hatred has in fact been stirred up, merely that it was either intended or likely to be stirred up.' This means someone can fall foul of the law for staging a play that does not stir up hatred and was never intended to stir up hatred but is considered 'likely' to stir up hatred by the CPS:

'The stirring up offences rather concern the use of words or behaviour, or the dissemination or possession (with a view to dissemination) of material which is intended to stir up racial hatred or hatred on grounds of religion or sexual orientation, or likely to stir up racial hatred. The offences in section 23 and 29G of the POA 1986 refer to such material as "inflammatory material" and we adopt this terminology, which we believe rightly reflects the harm involved: it is not that the material is offensive (though it may be); the rationale for criminalisation is that the material is likely to provoke angry or violent feelings.'[108]

The Law Commission outlines forms of conduct caught by the stirring up offences:

- Using threatening, abusive or insulting words or behaviour, or displaying written material which is threatening, abusive or insulting.

- Publishing or distributing written material which is threatening, abusive or insulting

- Presenting or directing the public performance of a play involving the use of threatening, abusive or insulting words or behaviour.

- Distributing, showing or playing a recording of visual images or sounds which are threatening, abusive or insulting.

- Providing a programme service, or producing or directing a programme, where the programme involves threatening, abusive or insulting visual images or sounds, or using the offending words or behaviour therein.

- Possessing written material, or a recording of visual images or sounds, which is threatening, abusive or insulting, with a view to it being displayed, published, distributed, shown, played or included in a cable programme service.

One problem with this is that, as previously noted, a subjective element is introduced into the law. There can be no objective definition of 'threatening, abusive or insulting.' What is considered insulting or offensive to one person may be considered funny to another or impassioned to a third person. The state is being asked to make judgements about our sensitivities and censor accordingly.

Yet the Law Commission gives such concerns short shrift:

'These offences attract a disproportionate amount of attention and controversy but in practice, there are very few prosecutions for stirring up offences and the threshold for a successful prosecution is high: "hatred" is more than mere hostility, or ridicule, or offence.'

Despite such protestations, journalist Darren Grimes and historian David Starkey were contacted by the police in October 2020 regarding Grimes' interview of Starkey for his *YouTube* channel conducted in June of that year. Starkey told Grimes that: 'Slavery was not genocide, otherwise there wouldn't be so many damned blacks in Africa or in Britain, would there?' This is a nasty, racist remark for which Starkey has since apologised. Grimes asks questions, nods, and published the exchange on his *YouTube* channel. Precisely which of these actions was considered to be 'stirring up racial hatred' is unclear. Although the charge has now been dropped, if found guilty under the Public Order Act 1986, the pair could have faced up to seven years in jail. The very fact of being questioned by police for expressing and publishing an opinion – however repellent – chills free expression.

In looking to expand the remit of 'stirring up offences' the Law Commission focuses particular attention upon 'the proliferation of damaging forms of hatred online,' noting that 'while some of the worst forms of such hatred may fall within one of the offences of stirring up hatred, abusive or offensive communications falling short of stirring up hatred are commonly prosecuted as one of the "communications offences"'. They argue that it would be 'logical' to add these offences 'to the regime of aggravated offences.'

The push to expand hate speech legislation is not necessarily driven by a desire to prosecute more people, but rather by a need for the law to send the 'correct' message about the nature of the offence committed. One motivation for the proposed reforms is that:

> 'if inflammatory material which does not amount to a display or recording is distributed – for instance, by the posting of inflammatory cartoons online – it may not be caught by the existing legislation. It may be possible to bring a prosecution under separate legislation – for instance the offence of sending by means of a public electronic communications network a message or other matter that is grossly offensive under section 127(1) of the Communications Act 2003. However, this does not carry the same gravity or labelling as the stirring up offences. It does not reflect the fundamental harm involved, which is not that it is offensive, but that it incites hatred.'[109]

In January 2015, 12 people were murdered and 11 others injured in a terrorist attack at the offices of the French satirical magazine *Charlie Hebdo*. Islamist terrorists sought to avenge the magazine for featuring cartoons of the prophet Mohammed. Their act sent a broader message that satirising Islam and portraying images of Mohammed is punishable by death. In October 2020, a French school teacher, Samuel Paty, was brutally murdered by an Islamist terrorist after he showed his students the Charlie Hebdo cartoons in a class on the importance of free speech. The Law Commission's proposals, and indeed their choice of example – *the posting of inflammatory cartoons online* – shows that in the UK, free expression will be policed by the state on behalf of Islamists. Potential terrorists see that violent acts lead to reward, in this case the reintroduction of blasphemy law, albeit under a different name.

The all-encompassing nature of the Law Commission's proposals is made clear:

> 'We provisionally propose a single offence of disseminating inflammatory material, based on the existing sections 23 and 29G of the Public Order Act 1986, which would explicitly, but not exhaustively, include: (1) written and other material; (2) plays and other staged performances; (3) television and radio broadcasts; (4) distribution and exhibition of film, sound and video recordings; (5) video games; and (6) online material. We provisionally propose that this offence should be distinct from the "use of words or behaviour" offence currently in sections 18 and 29B of the Public Order Act 1986.'[110]

The Law Commission calls for a particular focus on inflammatory material spread on social media, citing a 2017 report by the House of Commons Home Affairs Committee which found that it was 'shockingly easy to find examples of material that was intended to stir up hatred against ethnic minorities on all three of the social media platforms that we examined – *YouTube*, Twitter and Facebook.' They conclude:

> 'If social media companies are capable of using technology immediately to remove material that breaches copyright, they should be capable of using similar content to stop extremists re-posting or sharing illegal material under a different name. We believe that the Government should now assess whether the continued publication of illegal material and the failure to take reasonable steps to identify or remove it is in breach of the law, and how the law and enforcement mechanisms should be strengthened in this area.'[111]

Not only does the Law Commission propose the policing of all forms of communication, it also calls for more groups to be protected by 'stirring up' offences. It calls for protection to cover race, religion, sexual orientation, transgender identity, disability and women. At the same time, their Consultation Paper argues that:

> 'it would be possible to replace the offences in sections 18 and 29B with a single offence of unlawfully stirring up hatred, with the definition of "hatred" listing not only each of the current and proposed characteristics, but also hatred against a group defined by a combination of more than one characteristic.'

The Law Commission does propose maintaining existing protections for free speech within stirring up offences, noting that:

- The law applies to hatred against persons, not against institutions or belief systems;

- Criticism of behaviour is permitted;

- Maintaining a space for discussion of public policy on potentially controversial issues.

In addition, it proposes adding new exemptions 'to address potential issues which might arise as a result of expanding the scope of the stirring up offences' such as:

- The discussion or criticism of physical or behavioural differences relating to sex or gender;

- The discussion or criticism of gender reassignment and treatment for gender dysphoria;

- The provision of and access to single-sex facilities and activities.

Unlike prohibitions on expression which are defined loosely and broadly, protections on free speech are narrow and specific. For free expression to be meaningful, we would expect the exact opposite to be the case and for the presumption to be that anything can be said other than a very small number of narrow and tightly defined exceptions. Instead, if the Law Commission's proposals are passed into law, it will be presumed that nothing can be said other than that which is expressly permitted.

Policing our private lives

The Law Commission reject the suggestion that designating some offences as hate crimes 'amounts to the introduction of a category of thought crime'. They argue that this is not the case because 'every hate crime involves an action as well as a mental state. The law does not punish a neo-Nazi for his or her beliefs, but if those beliefs lead him or her to attack someone Jewish or desecrate a mosque, then the law rightly steps in.' However, when it comes to incitement and 'stirring up' offences, the only action is one of communication. Hate crime legislation may not make thought a crime, but it does prohibit the communication of certain thoughts. This means we are free to think, but not free to share our ideas with other people.

Furthermore, the Law Commission is concerned that when people express their thoughts, their words may not reflect the true content of their mind. They may be driven by hatred and hostility, even though they use no words that are explicitly abusive or insulting. This, they argue, 'creates a loophole' that enables 'organised groups, such as the far-right,' to make statements 'which would amount to an offence under the existing provisions', but cunningly 'limit their conduct accordingly, so as not to become criminally liable.' Rather than celebrating the success of legislation that pushes people to limit hateful conduct, the Law Commission wants legislation extended to capture the not-explicitly-articulated hateful intention behind the statements:

> 'Under our proposal, intentionally stirring up hatred would be an offence regardless of whether the words used were "threatening", or "abusive or insulting". The prosecution would be required to prove to the criminal standard that the words had been used with intent to stir up hatred. Of course, in many cases, the language used would be strong evidence of the speaker or writer's intent. However, there might be cases where despite using apparently moderate language, there is other evidence available to prove that the person did so with a demonstrable intention to stir up hatred.'[112]

The law not only moves into more subjective terrain, but also loses focus on the objective evidence. Presumably, group memberships and previous communications will be used as evidence of intent not found in the words being prosecuted. This certainly comes close to 'the introduction of a category of thought crime'.

As well as expressing concern that hate crime legislation may not capture people who are motivated by hostility but avoid the use of threatening language, the Law Commission is also concerned about those who do *not* intend to stir up hatred but come to the attention of the police because it is considered that they should have known that their words were 'likely to' stir up hatred. The Commission proposes replacing the 'likely to' limb with 'knew or ought to have known'. Under this formulation, there would be no need for a court to prove the defendant had knowledge or belief; 'culpable self-induced ignorance, whether because of intoxication or turning a blind eye, would give no defence'; and it would 'permit an organisation complicit in the distribution of inflammatory material to be prosecuted if it should have had procedures in place to identify and prevent the distribution of such material, but did not.' The shift from 'likely to' to 'knew or ought to have known' in relation to stirring up hatred is recommended on the basis of offering greater protection for free speech, but it is difficult to see how this is the case. Instead, it again allows the law to pass judgement on the (presumed) workings of people's minds as it seeks to determine what defendants know.

The Law Commission's Consultation proposes using hate crime legislation to extend the remit of the law further into our private lives. The Commission expresses concern that the Public Order Act 1986, though altering the Dwelling Exception so that words or behaviour intended or likely to incite racial hatred could be prosecuted if uttered in the private sphere, did not go far enough. An exception still permits words, behaviour or written material intended or likely to incite racial or religious hatred or hatred on grounds of sexual orientation to be used or displayed within a dwelling, as long as they cannot be seen or heard outside that or another dwelling. In other words, in the privacy of their own homes, people remain free to say whatever they like, no matter the likelihood of it inciting hatred, on condition that their words are not seen or heard by anyone outside of their home. The Commission proposes removing the dwelling exception entirely from the stirring up offences.

The Law Commission also wants to extend section 3 of the Football (Offences) Act 1991 on engaging in 'chanting of an indecent or racialist nature at a designated football match' to cover homophobic chanting. They acknowledge concern that 'not only is homophobic chanting extremely harmful to fans but it has a significant impact on players – it creates a culture of hostility which makes players feel they are unable able to come out and "be themselves"', and 'can create a hostile environment for spectators who possess those protected characteristics.'

The Law Commission's proposals would, if passed, see the law extend into every area of a person's life – including all forms of communication and conversations that take place within our own homes. We may be tried and found guilty of stirring up hatred, not on the basis of our actions, or even on the basis of our speech, but on the knowledge deemed to lie behind our speech.

Contempt for citizens

Using hate crime legislation to move from a concept of equality before the law towards an identitarian focus on recognition and affirmation results in individuals being viewed differently depending upon group membership. One group in particular is not covered by any of the categories considered worthy of additional legal protections. White, heterosexual, cis-gendered men are the only people not to fall into any one of the proposed protected characteristics. Indeed, white males are most likely presumed to be the perpetrators of hate crime.

The Law Commission notes: 'the majority of hate crime offenders in the UK are white, male and under 25'. Cited is a Welsh government report which indicated that '83.3% of all hate crime defendants across all monitored strands were men; 73.7% were categorised as 'white British'; and 26.3% identified as a category other than white.' Research is drawn upon that points to perpetrators being from 'families with a lack of formal education' and with 'life stories characterised by deprivation, mental health problems, domestic violence, drug and alcohol issues, and patterns of criminal behaviour.' This offender profiling helps in the creation of laws designed to protect people from young, white, working class men and, in turn, to re-educate this cohort about the correct way to treat members of supposedly oppressed groups.

The other common feature of many hate crimes is that they are not committed by strangers: 'in a third of cases the perpetrators had been known to victims either as acquaintances, neighbours, friends, work colleagues, family members or carers.' One problem the Law Commission seeks to tackle through changes to hate crime legislation is hostility in personal relationships. The Consultation describes: 'derision and contempt for disabled people', 'behaviour directed at disabled people out of a belief (whether true or not) that the victim's disability makes them an easier target – for example for financial or sexual exploitation', as well as 'the exploitation and abuse that older people too often experience'. This presents a desultory picture of intimate relationships shaped by prejudice and abuse. Legal changes are necessary to protect citizens from each other and to control and suppress our worst instincts.

Proposed changes in the law are more likely to target, and potentially criminalise, one particular social demographic, and also to pave the way for greater policing of interpersonal relationships. British law works on an assumption that citizens are innocent until proven guilty. One problem with premising legal changes on a view of one section of society as exploitative and prejudiced is that it calls into question this fundamental legal premise.

The Law Commission's Consultation Paper risks dividing citizens into those considered likely perpetrators of hate crimes versus those considered likely victims. The mirror image of the contempt for prejudiced and hostile likely-perpetrators is a degraded view of people thought likely to become victims.

One of the most obvious ways in which hate crime legislation degrades victims, or people thought likely to become victims, is through labelling them according to 'immutable characteristics' and treating them primarily as group members rather than as individuals. As the Law Commission's Consultation makes clear, this focus on group membership over individual characteristics is fundamental to the entire concept of hate crime. The rationale for hate crime law is that 'the harm caused by the crime is not limited to the affected individual, but impacts more broadly on people who share the characteristic to which the offender's hostility was directed, and the wider community to which the victims belong.' In other words, it is harm brought upon the wider social group, as much as harm to one specific victim, that is a punishable offence. One impact of this approach is to reduce crime victims to the biological demarcations that afford them group membership.

The Commission presents some groups as in need of additional protection, not just because they are more likely to experience prejudice and discrimination, but because of the way in which they are presumed likely to respond hate crimes committed against anyone else who shares their characteristics. The harm of hate speech, the Law Commission declares, 'is that it undermines the "public good" of the assurance of vulnerable groups in society that they will not be discriminated against, subjected to violence and experience subsequent feelings of anxiety and distress.' Not only does this assume one emotional response, 'anxiety and distress', it also assumes it is the role of the law to protect people from these feelings.

The Consultation cites research that emphasises 'the unique "emotional and psychological" harm caused by hate speech to groups which have been "historically oppressed, victimised, persecuted or systematically discriminated against".' This emotional and psychological harm, we are told, can lead to anger: 'emotions of anger can particularly impact secondary victims in LGBT and Muslim communities.' One reason given for this is the 'strong empathic connections that arise out of shared experiences in these respective communities, including shared experiences of victimisation and discrimination.' An alternative way to interpret this statement is that some groups in society are less in control of their emotional responses and are more prone to outbursts of anger than others.

Although appearing to be sympathetic, arguments around group emotional responses present some people as less rational and more volatile. In response, punishment for the perpetrators of hate crime is needed so as to provide a 'societal safety valve': 'a safe and institutionally controlled avenue for those affected by crimes to release their ill-will and/or desire for revenge.' This suggestion that hate crime legislation is needed to prevent certain victims taking the law into their own hands is a form of blackmail. It degrades victims to suggest they may be overtaken by urges they are unable to control.

Identity politics

The Law Commission's Consultation is shaped by identity politics and CLT. We have already noted the emphasis on categorising people into groups determined by 'immutable characteristics.' Immutable characteristics are features about a person they have no control over, such as skin colour, age, sex and disability. Gender identity and sexuality are also considered to be immutable characteristics. One problem with defining identity in this way is that it reduces people to their biology. The Consultation Paper suggests:

'A more nuanced approach than "immutability" might be to focus on characteristics that are considered fundamental to personal identity. Protection of religious belief fits much more neatly within this framework, alongside race, gender identity and sexual orientation.'

In this way, the law is brought in line with current thinking in relation to identity politics and its positioning of identity above social class in determining social power relations.

Hate crime becomes defined as any act that specifically targets someone on the basis of their identity: 'hate crime is an attack upon a core part of the victim's identity.' This is particularly the case for groups where their identity is 'already a source of disadvantage' and the crime committed against them compounds the harm experienced. As previously noted in relation to sex, race and transgender, the broader framing of hate crime within the context of identity politics means that the harm suffered is presented less as a matter concerning individuals and more as an injury to the entire group. It 'impacts more broadly on people who share the characteristic to which the offender's hostility was directed, and the wider community to which the victims belong.' This means that the circumstances of an individual victim are irrelevant; if the group to which they belong is considered to have been historically oppressed or is still disadvantaged then the harm of the original crime is compounded to such an extent that it falls under the jurisdiction of the law.

Identity politics compels both victim and perpetrator to be seen, in the eyes of the law, as representatives of a group that shares the same immutable characteristics rather than as individuals with agency over their own lives. Hate crime becomes seen as the exercise of power, the means by which 'the majority group' keeps 'the minority group in a subordinate position.' This view derives from a Foucauldian view of crime that situates individual actions within a broader context of structural power relations. The Law Commission cite academics who argue that hate crime

'...is a mechanism of power and oppression, intended to reaffirm the precarious hierarchies that characterise a given social order. It attempts to re-create simultaneously the threatened (real or imagined) hegemony of the perpetrator's group and the "appropriate" subordinate identity of the victim's group. It is a means of marking both the Self and the Other in such a way as to re-establish their "proper" relative positions, as given and reproduced by broader ideologies and patterns of social and political inequality.'

There are problems with applying this structural understanding to the law. When victims and perpetrators are seen as identity group members, no allowance is made for their individual circumstances. For example, a black female will be viewed as more disadvantaged than a white male. But when the black female is a wealthy, well-educated lawyer while the white male has no qualifications and is unemployed, it is difficult to see the latter as inherently less powerful. Identity politics rarely takes account of social class or wealth differentials. When it does, class becomes just one more facet of an individual's identity, rather than the most fundamental determining factor of their life chances. Finally, the turn towards identity absolves both victim and perpetrator of responsibility for their own actions and responses.

The authors of the Law Commission Consultation on Hate Crime are so wedded to CLT they cannot account for these problems with their approach. Instead, they point to issues that confirm, rather than challenge, their underlying thesis. For example, they note difficulties in accounting for 'the intersectional nature of victims' characteristics.' They define 'intersectional' as meaning 'the fact that some people experience multiple and overlapping forms of discrimination and abuse – for example, lesbian women may experience both misogyny and homophobia, and sometimes both at the same time.' They point to research suggesting that groups such as Muslim women who 'felt targeted because they were visibly Muslim, and also because as women, there was a perception they were less likely to fight back.' Applying intersectionality to identity politics does not stop reducing people to group membership, it simply narrows the groups to which people are assigned.

The objective nature of the crime committed against a person does not change because the victim is a member of more than one oppressed group. By emphasising the importance of intersectionality, the Law Commission acknowledges that one key purpose of hate crime legislation is to afford recognition to victims of the harm suffered and, significantly, to affirm the 'worth' of their identity group. The importance of affirmation and recognition underpin the focus, not just on punishing the perpetrators of hate crime, but on the detailed recording of non-crime hate incidents: 'limitations to reflecting intersectionality in law should not, however, prevent the appropriate police recording of intersectional hate crimes, nor the provision of appropriate support based on multiple forms of targeting.'

Law as therapy
When the law is concerned with affirming identity, there is no limit on the number of groups seeking recognition. The Law Commission's Consultation Paper notes 'groups which are targeted for certain crime types, but are not currently

recognised as protected characteristics for the purposes of hate crime' and lists:

- Women;
- Older people;
- Homeless people;
- Sex workers;
- Members of alternative subcultures (later specified as: goths, emos, punks, metallers and some variants of hippie and dance culture – although this list is not exhaustive);
- Those who adhere to non-religious philosophical beliefs.

Elsewhere, the report discusses the need to recognise asexual orientation, 'the experience of not being sexually attracted to others.' According to the Consultation, '1% of the population has this orientation', and this is sufficient for the Law Commission to consider that 'there is now a stronger case for asexuality to have the same level of protection as other forms of orientation – attraction to the same sex, opposite sex or both.' They propose a revised definition that refers to: 'a group of persons defined by reference to sexual orientation, whether towards persons of the same sex, the opposite sex, both or neither.'

One solution to this growing demand for recognition might be to move to a more individualised, case-by-case consideration of hate crime, taking account of all evidence of hostility as a motivating and aggravating factor for a crime. However, the Law Commission pushes back against this proposal arguing that specifying protected characteristics is preferable because:

- It recognises that certain groups in society experience more severe harms as a result of being targeted for criminal behaviour than others.

- It provides a legal basis for responding to these forms of harm.

- It makes the law more certain and comprehensible.

- It reduces the risk of perverse outcomes, whereby the law provides enhanced legal protection to groups whose actions have been recognised as harmful in other contexts: for example, terrorist organisations and sex offenders.

The Law Commission proposes to increase the specific groups protected by hate crime legislation. Limiting the number of 'places available,' in this way, leads to a competition for legal recognition with the Law Commission as arbiter over claims for inclusion. So, we learn, for example, that Humanists argued that 'groups that hold philosophical beliefs that are not religious in nature' should be recognised as a protected characteristic for the purposes of hate crime, while The Sophie Lancaster Foundation argued for recognition of '"alternative subcultures" such as goths and punks'.

Groups try to outbid each other in demonstrating the extent of their suffering. For example, research is highlighted suggesting 'that those who belong to alternative subcultures experience harassment and abuse which has the effect of othering them.' Details include: 'insults such as 'freak!', derogatory forms of humour, direct accusatory questions, demands, threats and one incident where a goth was told to go 'slit their wrists and die'.' This has an impact upon members' 'sense of self-worth, self-confidence, security and psychological wellbeing.' Meanwhile, concern is expressed that recognising 'crime based on prejudice or hostility towards people experiencing homelessness might entrench the stigma that this group already experiences' and 'reinforce the outsider status of this group and cause further isolation and withdrawal – undermining their equality in society.'[113]

The Law Commission appears to encourage this competition, and clarifies the rules of the game. They suggest group members:

'might argue that they experience greater harm as a result of the criminal behaviour because it targets; (1) A characteristic that was an important aspect of their identity or, (2) A characteristic on the basis of which they experience disadvantage. A person might show that the characteristic was central to their identity in various nonexhaustive ways. For example, they might point to the fact that:

- The characteristic is immutable, or they have little or no control over the fact they have the characteristic.

- The characteristic significantly influences their lived experience of the world.

- Society places significant emphasis on the characteristic. (This might include socially constituted identities based on the characteristic, or the fact that certain groups can have their overall identity reduced to the characteristic).

- Sharing this characteristic gives rise to a strong sense of collective identity.'

They further specify:

'Disadvantage could be defined with reference to systemic conditions that negatively impact, or have historically negatively impacted, certain groups because of a characteristic they share. The reference to "systemic" disadvantage is important here – it is the fact that hate crime can replicate or invoke aspects of wider, systemic disadvantage on a micro level that arguably contributes to the additional harm caused to victims in individual cases. Some examples of relevant systemic conditions might be:

- violence or abuse towards the characteristic group which is commonplace or normalised

- discrimination that is ingrained in prominent institutions, or in widespread social norms
- social exclusion or marginalisation of members of the characteristic group
- widely held stigma related to the characteristic.'

The need to specify criteria for inclusion in hate crime protections is driven by an acknowledgement that what is at stake is primarily symbolic. There is concern that if hate crime offences against a particular group are consistently not proven in court, then this 'could prove more harmful than helpful in symbolic terms for the characteristic to be added.' The Law Commission expresses concern that convictions 'not labelled in a formal sense as a hate crime' do 'not carry the same symbolic and denunciatory impact as an aggravated version of the offence.' In practice, they suggest, this means that under current protocol,

'groups who are protected by enhanced sentencing alone (LGBT and disabled victims) feel that the harm they experience is treated as lesser. This contributes to a perception that they are second class citizens in the eyes of the law, damaging trust and confidence in the criminal justice system.'

In this way, the law comes to serve a therapeutic purpose in affirming the identity of marginalised groups and publicly acknowledging members' hurt feelings. To this end, the Law Commission considers various therapeutic initiatives designed to be employed with both victims and offenders.

Restorative justice is described as 'an alternative or supplement to the retributive model of sentencing, with a focus on repairing the harms caused by hate crime'. Many restorative justice programmes aim to bring victims and offenders together for mediation. Sessions may 'explore the reasons behind why the offence was committed, the harms that it has caused to the victim and other stakeholders, the means by which the offender will repair the harms he or she has caused, and the reintegration of the offender into the community.' Two potentially beneficial outcomes are identified: 'challenge prejudice and heal victims'.

Out of Court Disposals (OOCDs) are intended to '"divert" minor and undisputed incidents away from the formal court process' – thereby reducing the time and expense involved in full legal proceedings. However, some OOCDs can demand a greater commitment from 'offenders' who are denied a formal opportunity to clear their name. Educational and rehabilitation programmes can form part of OOCD, such as *Think Again*, 'a ten-session intervention programme which was implemented in West Yorkshire in 2010.' Attendance can be a conditional requirement of community orders. If convicted and sentenced, offenders can be made to undergo prison-based rehabilitation programmes, such as *Diversity Awareness Prejudice Pack* (DAPP). DAPP began in 2001 to deal with racist hate offending and developed to tackle 'disablist and homophobic hate offending'. DAPP 'aims to reduce hate crime reoffending by addressing deeply entrenched prejudices. It asks offenders to reflect on this and how their beliefs formed'. A similar programme, *Promoting Human Dignity*, aims 'to tackle racist hate reoffending,' particularly 'hatred toward refugees and migrants as forms of racism.' Weekly sessions cover: 'labelling discrimination; the impact of racist offending on victims and developing alternative attitudes and behaviours.'

Historically, the law has been concerned with objective harms that can be evidenced in a court. It has stood above the feelings of victims and the opinions of offenders. A crime was a crime irrespective of how either party felt about it. Over recent decades this has changed. Victim impact statements are now heard in court. Hate crime legislation introduces subjective definitions of harm in which the perception and feelings of the victim form the basis of a criminal offence and the views expressed, if not the intention, of the perpetrator are punished. The legal system comes to play a role that is both therapeutic and political and the Law Commission's proposed changes take us further in this direction.

Promoting values

The Law Commission's proposals use hate crime legislation to transform the law into a therapeutic tool of the state, intervening in citizens' interpersonal relationships and arbitrating competing claims to victimhood. In addition to this, hate crime legislation is expected to play a didactic role, re-educating not just individual offenders, but sending a message to the wider community about acceptable behaviour, language and attitudes. Presumably, it is the authors of the Law Commission Consultation Paper, as well as the many academics and representatives from campaigning organisations cited, who get to determine the behaviour, language and attitudes deemed acceptable.

The consultation paper, firmly rooted within identity politics, echoes the concerns of a politically and socially homogeneous elite. For example, one prominent call is to 'recognise misogynistic criminal behaviour as a form of hate crime'. Many older working-class women are far more likely to be concerned with low pay and working conditions than they are by 'verbal and non-verbal street remarks'. Yet the Law Commission focuses on misogynistic hate crime 'in order to recognise the extent and unacceptability of this behaviour'. The law is being used to send a message to the population about the correct way to treat women. As the paper states clearly: 'misogyny hate crime has declaratory importance; it would put down 'a marker to say that culturally endemic negative attitudes towards women are not acceptable'.'

One particular concern is with the proliferation of 'rape myths'. The Law Commission notes that, 'after a bias incident, there is often discussion about the crime that serves to educate the public. If sexual assaults were appropriately labelled as hate crimes, a similar discussion could occur in regard to rape and other forms of gender-motivated violence that would educate the public about the actual nature of rape and discredit common rape myths.' This may well be true, but it moves us a long way from simply punishing offenders.

The educative function of hate speech laws is explained: 'the regulation of hate speech can lead to greater consciousness in society about the negative impact of such conduct toward vulnerable groups.' But, to some of the academics cited by the Law Commission, 'vulnerable groups' can usefully be exploited for the promotion of a particular political outlook. They express concern that hate crime challenges 'long and deeply held values of inclusion, equity, and justice' and that it can damage 'shared values of equality'. Hate speech legislation, on the other hand, 'can signal the boundaries of acceptable behaviour which helps to create a 'well-ordered' society fostering greater social interaction and cohesion,' as well as upholding, 'equality and civility'. The political role of hate crime law is made explicit:

> 'hate crime laws also serve an important symbolic function in tackling bigotry, prejudice and inequality, and affirming the identity and personhood of those who are subjected to it [...] this links with a broader equality movement in contemporary society, which seeks to redress traditional sources of discrimination'.

The authors do not specify why the law should be used in favour of their preferred political objectives. Indeed, the values specified are not seen as 'political' at all, but merely the representative of the outlook shared by all right-thinking people.

The Law Commission proposes the establishment of a national Hate Crime Commissioner whose key functions 'might be to encourage good practice in the prevention, detection, investigation and prosecution of offences associated with hate crime, as well as the identification of victims and perpetrators of these offences.' Additional responsibilities, we are told, might include:

- Support the development and implementation of relevant educational resources which challenge the prejudicial attitudes that underpin hate crime.

- Raise awareness of the prevalence and specific impacts of hate crime on individuals and communities more widely, through media, social media and speaking opportunities.

- Conduct centralised consultation with a diverse range of stakeholders who represent the views of affected parties across all hate crime strands.

- Co-operate and consult with other Commissioners, such as the Victims' Commissioner, Domestic Abuse Commissioner, or the Lead Commissioner for Counter Extremism on areas which overlap.

This appears to be a role more akin to that of a campaign manager than a legal representative or crime-fighter.

The role, we are further informed, 'may also help to raise the profile of hate crime in communities, and encourage confidence in victims coming forward and reporting hate crimes and incidents.' One thing is for sure, a hate crime commissioner will never be out of work. The more awareness is raised about hate crime, the more people come to perceive themselves as victims and look to the police and the judiciary for confirmation of their suffering. The path is cleared for a never-ending cycle of awareness raising, increased reporting and community intervention. The upshot is a society in which equality before the law and freedom of expression are both jettisoned in order to affirm selected identity groups.

Conclusions

Hate crime legislation has, over the course of several decades, expanded to offer protections to more groups of people and to criminalise an increasing range of speech and behaviour. Hate speech falls under the Communications Act, the Football Offences Act and branches of the Public Order and Criminal Justice Acts. In addition, offensive words and behaviour that fall short of being a criminal offence are recorded as non-crime hate incidents. The impact of multiple pieces of legislation and police guidance is to curtail and chill free expression.

Each new Act of Parliament and clarification of police guidance introduces a more subjective element into the law. The state, either through the CPS or the police, comes to define what is offensive, threatening or abusive. Such understandings are grounded in a perception of the 'lived experiences' of 'victims' as members of historically oppressed groups and a belief that words can have an impact as harmful as an act of physical violence. Identity groups are represented by 'hate crime entrepreneurs' who are incentivised to report ever increasing harms experienced by members of their community. The law comes to play a role in affirming the identity of victim groups, recognising suffering, re-educating offenders about the 'correct' way to think and sending a message to the rest of society about the values deemed 'appropriate'.

The Law Commission's Consultation on Hate Crime Law, like the Hate Crime and Public Order (Scotland) Bill, are grounded in CLT. This assumes that equality before the law is not only insufficient to achieving social equality, but is an active barrier to social justice. According to this view, legal equality consolidates historical inequities. This draws upon a perception of citizens as members of identity groups whose lives are forever shaped by history and biology and a perception of the law as needed to protect historically oppressed groups and to promote social justice in the present. This is contemptuous of citizens who are divided into victims and perpetrators based on supposedly 'immutable' characteristics.

If passed into law, the Law Commission's hate crime proposals will erode the concept of equality before the law and curtail free expression. Every aspect of people's lives will come under legal scrutiny in order to promote a set of state sanctioned values that have been determined by lawyers rather than voted on by the electorate. In the interests of individual freedom, personal autonomy and equality before the law, the Law Commission's proposals, as well as existing hate crime laws and guidance, must be challenged.

Recommendations

- There should be no extensions to existing hate speech legislation.

- The police should neither formally question people accused of, nor keep records of, non-crime hate incidents.

- No 'characteristics' should receive special legal protection in a way that violates the principle of equality under the law.

- Curtail the influence of hate crime entrepreneurs. Groups with a vested interest in presenting their members as victims of hate crime should not influence hate crime legislation.

- Hold an inquiry to determine, review and potentially repeal all elements of the law that conflict with freedom of speech, for example: Section 127 of the Communications Act, offences of stirring up hatred under the Public Order Act 1986, and the offence of 'indecent or racialist chanting' under the Football (Offences) Act 1991.

Notes

1   London bus attack: Boys told couple 'to show how lesbians have sex'
2   Homophobic hate crime in UK almost trebled since 2014, new figures show
3   Hate crime, England and Wales, 2018 to 2019
4   Report hate crime - GOV.UK
5   Hate crime laws A consultation paper
6   Hate crime laws A consultation paper
7   What is hate crime? | The Met
8   Protected characteristics
9   Hate incidents aren't the same as hate crimes
10   Hate crime
11   What is hate crime? | The Met
12   What is hate crime? | The Met
13   CPS calls for 'corrosive' online hate crime to be taken more seriously
14   Hate crime laws A consultation paper
15   The Blasphemies of Thomas Aikenhead
16   Blasphemy, Cultural Divergence and Legal Relativism
17   Hate Speech, Incitement to Hatred and Sexual Orientation in England, Wales and Northern Ireland
18   Hate Speech, Incitement to Hatred and Sexual Orientation in England, Wales and Northern Ireland
19   Oxford Pro Bono Publico COMPARATIVE HATE SPEECH LAW: ANNEXURE
20   http://www.austlii.edu.au/au/journals/AJHR/1994/15.html#fn44
21   Human Rights Act 1998
22   THE STEPHEN LAWRENCE INQUIRY
23   https://commonslibrary.parliament.uk/research-briefings/cdp-2019-0052/#:~:text=The%20Macpherson%20Report%20was%20published,of%20leadership%20by%20senior%20officers%E2%80%9D.

24   HATE CRIME: THE CASE FOR EXTENDING THE EXISTING OFFENCES

25   Harmful Online Communications: The Criminal Offences A Consultation paper

26   Hate Crime Operational Guidance

27   Hate crime, England and Wales, 2018 to 2019

28   Online Hate Crime Hub | Mayor's Question Time

29   Hate Crime Operational Guidance

30   New national hate crime guidance published

31   Hate Crime and Public Order (Scotland) Bill

32   Crime prevention: Hate crime - gov.scot

33   Hate crime laws A consultation paper

34   Protected characteristics

35   Equality Act 2010

36   Age discrimination

37   The New Single Equality Act in Britain

38   Interview with author

39   Hate crime laws A consultation paper

40   Hate crime, England and Wales, 2018 to 2019

41   Hate crime, England and Wales, 2018 to 2019

42   Second woman is investigated by police over transphobic comments

43   Hate crime, England and Wales, 2018 to 2019

44   Brexit 'major influence' in racism and hate crime rise

45   Hate crime, England and Wales, 2018 to 2019

46   Hate crime, England and Wales, 2017 to 2018

47   Hate crime, England and Wales, 2017 to 2018

48   Hate crime, England and Wales, 2017 to 2018

49   Hate crime, England and Wales, 2018 to 2019

50   Hate Crime Report 2018-2019

51   Hate crime action plan: Challenge it, Report it, Stop it

52   HATE CRIME: THE CASE FOR EXTENDING THE EXISTING OFFENCES

53   Harmful Online Communications: The Criminal Offences A Consultation paper

54   Online Harms White Paper - GOV.UK

55   Hate crime laws A consultation paper

56   http://www.lawcom.gov.uk/app/uploads/2015/03/cp213_hate_crime_amended.pdf

57   HATE CRIME: THE CASE FOR EXTENDING THE EXISTING OFFENCES

58 Action Against Hate. The UK Government's plan for tackling hate crime

59 https://assets.publishing.service.gov.uk/government/uploads/system/uploads/attachment_data/file/543679/Action_Against_Hate_-_UK_Government_s_Plan_to_Tackle_Hate_Crime_2016.pdf

60 Hate crime laws A consultation paper

61 Amber Rudd speech on foreign workers recorded as hate incident

62 Amber Rudd speech on foreign workers recorded as hate incident

63 Harry Miller

64 https://www.bbc.co.uk/news/uk-england-lincolnshire-51501202

65 Hate-crime-judicial-review-statement-February-2020

66 Hate-crime-judicial-review-statement-February-2020

67 Hate-crime-judicial-review-statement-February-2020

68 National Black Police Association – National Black Police Association

69 https://www.nbpa.co.uk/wp-content/uploads/2020/05/31-05-2020-NBPA-Statement-Murder-of-George-Floyd-.pdf

70 The National LGBT Police Network – Representative body for LGBT Police groups

71 https://lgbt.police.uk/wp-content/uploads/2020/04/TG-Overview.pdf

72 https://lgbt.police.uk/wp-content/uploads/2020/04/TG-Overview.pdf

73 Members of Stonewall's Diversity Champions programme

74 A practical guide for police forces

75 Independent review of hate crime legislation in Scotland: final report - gov.scot

76 Could Scotland's hate crime bill make depictions of Mohammed illegal?

77 Lack of clarity in Hate Crime Bill could threaten freedom of expression

78 New Scottish hate crime laws 'could devastate legitimacy of police'

79 https://www.thetimes.co.uk/article/hate-speech-in-scotland-cry-freedom-to-jest-or-laugh-no-more-xffhtzxcq?shareToken=10b06898d0f21a2159752b5e452b9dbb

80 New Scottish hate crime laws 'could devastate legitimacy of police'

81 Controversial hate crime legislation to be changed

82 Interview with author

83 Interview with author

84 Interview with author

85 Hate crime laws A consultation paper

86   Hate crime laws A consultation paper
87   Hate crime laws A consultation paper
88   Hate crime laws A consultation paper
89   Misogyny is not a hate crime | Andrew Tettenborn
90   Misogyny is not a hate crime | Andrew Tettenborn
91   Hate crime laws A consultation paper
92   Toxic Twitter - A Toxic Place for Women
93   Hate crime laws A consultation paper
94   Hate crime laws A consultation paper
95   See, for example, The madness of our gender debate, where feminists defend slapping a 60-year-old woman
96   Hate crime laws A consultation paper
97   Hate crime laws A consultation paper
98   Hate crime laws A consultation paper
99   Hate crime laws A consultation paper
100 Hate crime laws A consultation paper
101 Hate crime laws A consultation paper
102 Hate crime laws A consultation paper
103 Critical Legal Theory | Wex | US Law | LII / Legal Information Institute
104 Hate crime laws A consultation paper
105 https://www.equalityhumanrights.com/en/human-rights-act/article-10-freedom-expression#:~:text=Article%2010%20of%20the%20Human%20Rights%20Act%3A%20Freedom%20of%20expression&text=This%20right%20shall%20include%20freedom,authority%20and%20regardless%20of%20frontiers.
106 Hate crime laws A consultation paper
107 Hate crime laws A consultation paper
108 Hate crime laws A consultation paper
109 Hate crime laws A consultation paper
110 Hate crime laws A consultation paper
111 Hate crime laws A consultation paper
112 Hate crime laws A consultation paper
113 Hate crime laws A consultation paper

CIVITAS

Our Aims and Programmes

- We facilitate informed public debate by providing accurate factual information on the social issues of the day, publishing informed comment and analysis, and bringing together leading protagonists in open discussion. Civitas never takes a corporate view on any of the issues tackled during the course of this work. Our current focus is on issues such as education, health, crime, social security, manufacturing, the abuse of human rights law, and the European Union.

- We ensure that there is strong evidence for all our conclusions and present the evidence in a balanced and objective way. Our publications are usually refereed by independent commentators, who may be academics or experts in their field.

- We strive to benefit public debate through independent research, reasoned argument, lucid explanation and open discussion. We stand apart from party politics and transitory intellectual fashions.

- Uniquely among think tanks, we play an active, practical part in rebuilding civil society by running schools on Saturdays and after-school hours so that children who are falling behind at school can achieve their full potential.

Subscriptions and Membership

For subscriptions and membership forms, go to:
https://www.civitas.org.uk/subscriptions-and-membership/
or call (0)20 7799 6677

Book Subscriptions – £35 a year (UK only): If you would like to stay abreast of Civitas' latest work, you can have all of our books delivered to your door as soon as they are published.

Friends of Civitas – £25 special offer for the first year (UK only): As a Friend of Civitas you will receive all of our publications – including not only our books but all online releases – throughout the year.

Renewals for Existing Members: If you are an existing member who has previously paid via cheque or using our internal form but would like to renew with the ease and convenience of PayPal, please access the link above.

Make a Donation: If you like our work and would like to help see it continue, please consider making a donation.

Supporters of Civitas: If you would like to support our work on a rolling basis, there is a variety of advanced membership levels on offer.

Forms can be either faxed to
+44 (0)20 7799 6688 or posted to:

Civitas: Institute For The Study Of Civil Society
First Floor
55 Tufton Street
Westminster
London
SW1P 3QL.

Please make cheques payable to Civitas.
Email: subs@civitas.org.uk

Civitas is a registered charity, No. 1085494